Women of Achievement

Marie Curie

Women of Achievement

Susan B. Anthony

Hillary Rodham Clinton

Marie Curie

Ellen DeGeneres

Nancy Pelosi

Rachael Ray

Eleanor Roosevelt

Martha Stewart

Women of Achievement

Marie Curie

SCIENTIST

Rachel A. Koestler-Grack

CHELSEA HOUSE
PUBLISHERS
An imprint of Infobase Publishing

MARIE CURIE

Chelsea House
An imprint of Infobase Publishing
132 West 31st Street
New York NY 10001

Library of Congress Cataloging-in-Publication Data
Koestler-Grack, Rachel A., 1973-
  Marie Curie : Scientist / Rachel A. Koestler-Grack.
     p. cm. — (Women of achievement)
  Includes bibliographical references and index.
  ISBN 978-1-60413-086-7 (hardcover)
  1. Curie, Marie, 1867-1934. 2. Chemists—Poland—Biography. 3. Women chemists—Poland—Biography. 4. Chemists—France—Biography. 5. Women chemists—France—Biography. I. Title. II. Series.

  QD22.C8K65 2009
  540.92—dc22
  [B]
                                    2008034999

Series design by Erik Lindstrom
Cover design by Ben Peterson

Printed in the United States of America

Bang EJB 10 9 8 7 6 5 4 3 2 1

This book is printed on acid-free paper.

CONTENTS

"Curie Cures Cancer!"

On May 12, 1921, the *Olympic* ocean liner docked at New York City. Almost at once, a frenzy of American reporters stampeded on deck, awaiting the appearance of Madame Curie, the famous French physicist and Nobel Prize winner. Before long, a frail, gray-haired woman stepped onto the deck, dressed in a loose black dress and a frumpy felt hat. Her two daughters stood next to her, one on each side. The publicity-shy Marie Curie was overwhelmed by the multitude of reporters rattling off questions. All around her flashbulbs popped, while an onshore band played three national anthems—French, Polish, and American. Curie shuffled over to a chair and sat down. She politely obeyed the reporters' instructions to look here or turn there and answered their questions in the flat, sterile tone of a true scientist.

At age 53, Curie was on her first trans-Atlantic trip to the United States. The journey was out of character for Curie—who preferred to stay hidden from the public eye. However, thanks to the dynamic and savvy Marie "Missy" Mattingly Meloney—editor of *The Delineator*, an American women's publication—Madame Curie was going to receive a special gift. Meloney had printed a series of articles on the life and career of Curie, France's most notable scientist— the woman who had discovered radium. The discovery was one of enormous weight, since radium had cancer-curing properties. Even though Curie was a Nobel Prize-winning scientist, she had little pure radium at her disposal for further research. Just a tiny gram of this precious element wore a price tag of $100,000.

Meloney's articles came at the right time in American history, just as women had earned the right to vote and the women's-rights movement was in full momentum. The story of a struggling female scientist appealed to American women of all social backgrounds. Most important, though, *The Delineator* gained the attention of prominent, wealthy women such as Grace Coolidge, the wife of Calvin Coolidge, who would become U.S. president in 1923; and Mrs. Robert Mead, founder of the American Society for the Control of Cancer. These women helped run a fund-raising campaign to buy Curie a gram of radium. Together with the women of America, they reached their goal within a year.

MISLEADING HEADLINE

The morning after Curie's arrival in New York, she awoke to this headline in *The New York Times*: "Mme Curie Plans to End All Cancers." The title was a misquote of a statement Curie had made the day before. The article quoted her as saying, "Radium is a positive cure for cancer. It has already cured all kinds of cancers, even deep-rooted cases."[1] What Curie actually said was that radium was a specific therapy for many forms of the disease, but it was not a cure for every cancer. *The New York Times* ran a retraction, but few people probably read it. The correction appeared on Page 16, the original article on Page 1.

Discovered in 1898, radium took the world by storm. Immediately after its discovery, Marie Curie and her husband, Pierre, performed experiments on the element's biological properties. The results suggested that radium could be used to cure diseases. Practically overnight, a new branch of medical science emerged called radium therapy. In France, this treatment was referred to as "Curie therapy." The first recorded successful use of radium treatments to cure cancer took place in Russia, not France, in 1903. In St. Petersburg, two patients suffering from basal cell carcinoma (or skin cancer) of the face received radium treatments and were cured. Naturally, the next step was to apply radium treatments to internal tissue. By 1904, the Curies were working with technicians and doctors to test radium on numerous illnesses, from cancer to tuberculosis. For the most part, the results were poor. Still, people insisted on using radium remedies. By 1913, Curie therapy with radium had been established as a specialty treatment for cancer, used on thousands in the United States and Europe each year.

The myth that radium would rid the world of cancer followed Marie Curie to the shores of New York in the spring of 1921. After eight days of tours and lectures, President Warren Harding presented her with her prize in an afternoon ceremony at the White House. One gram of pure radium rested in a lead-lined mahogany box. President Harding ceremoniously handed Curie a small golden key that would unlock the treasure—symbolically representing a key to the ultimate cure. To Americans, the United States could now claim a hand in eradicating the world of its most deadly disease. Curie, though, knew the

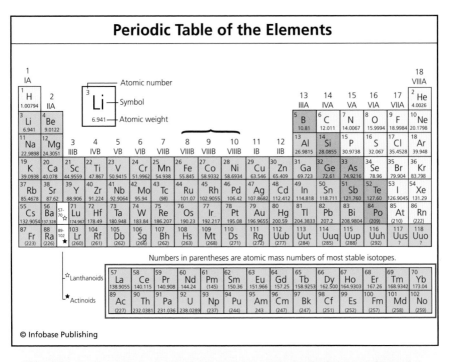

Elements are substances that cannot be chemically broken down into other substances. They are listed on the periodic table of the elements. Marie Curie and her husband, Pierre, discovered radium and polonium. Polonium (Po) has an atomic number of 84, and radium (Ra) has an atomic number of 88.

truth—the radium was to be used for research, not medicinal purposes.

Radium in medical cures is now obsolete, and the term Curie therapy has disappeared from medical journals. By the 1950s, cobalt and other related substances replaced radium. Cobalt 60, a radioactive isotope, offers a strong source of gamma rays and is therefore effective in treating cancers. In actuality, during this scientific era, an untold number of people suffered or died from exposure to radioactivity—including its parents, Pierre and Marie Curie. Nevertheless, Marie Curie's obsession with radium and

PERIODIC TABLE OF THE ELEMENTS

The periodic table of the elements hangs on the wall of nearly every chemistry classroom on the planet. At first glance, it merely looks like a series of boxes with letters and numbers in them, arranged in some kind of code. The boxes would form a rectangle, 18 across and 7 deep, but there are gaps in them, including two rows along the bottom separated from the rest of the chart. This table is more than just a simple chart, however. Created in 1869, it is one of the most sophisticated and usable means ever designed to represent complex interactions between the building blocks of matter.

Rows on the periodic table of the elements are called periods, and the columns are known as groups. Each box represents an element by its chemical symbol, along with its atomic number and its average atomic mass in units. An element is a substance that cannot be broken down chemically into another substance. The atom is the smallest particle of an element that retains all the chemical and physical properties of the element. Elements contain only one kind of atom. The atomic number represents the number of positive charges, or protons, in the nucleus of an atom. For example, carbon (with a chemical symbol of "C") has an atomic number of six, because it has six protons in the nucleus. Radium (or "Ra"), which Marie Curie discovered, has an atomic number of 88. In addition, each box also lists the average atomic mass of each element. For hydrogen (with the chemical symbol of "H"), the atomic mass is 1.00794.

As of 2008, there are 117 known elements, 90 of which occur naturally on Earth. Uranium, atomic number 92, was the last naturally occurring element to be discovered. Throughout time, the periodic table of the elements has continued, and still continues, to grow.

Marie Curie is seen conducting an experiment in her laboratory in Paris, France, in this 1925 photograph. Curie's discovery of radioactivity transformed the world, and her achievements helped to pave the way for other women working in the sciences.

radioactivity helped usher in a new era in scientific technology. Her discoveries remain among the greatest glories of modern science.

Curie's contributions also brought much-needed respect to women of all professions. She cleared a path so that other great women could follow her example. Because of her unconventional attitudes, many other women joined the fields of science and mathematics. In his speech on May 20, 1921, President Harding acknowledged these accomplishments as well as those she had achieved in science. He said:

As a nation whose womanhood has been exalted to fullest participation in citizenship, we are proud to honor in you a woman whose work has earned universal acclaim and attested woman's equality in every intellectual and spiritual activity. . . . We greet you as foremost among scientists in the age of science. . . .

In testimony of the affection of the American people, of their confidence in your scientific work, and of their earnest wish that your genius and energy may receive all encouragement to carry forward your efforts for the advance of science and conquest of disease, I have been commissioned to present to you this little phial of radium.

To you we owe our knowledge and possession of it, and so to you we give it, confident that in your possession it will be the means further to unveil the fascinating secrets of nature, to widen the field of useful knowledge, to alleviate suffering among the children of man. Take it to use as your wisdom shall direct and your purpose of service shall incline you. . . . It will remind you of the love of a grateful people for yourself; and it will testify in the useful work to which you devote it, the reverence of mankind for one of its foremost benefactors and most beloved of women.[2]

Manya:
A Brilliant Child

Four-year-old Marya Sklodowska, nicknamed Manya, stared into a locked glass cabinet as if in a trance. Strange and beautiful instruments had been packed onto several shelves. There were glass tubes, small scales, specimens of minerals, and even a gold-leaf electroscope. Little Manya asked Professor Wladyslaw Sklodowski what these graceful objects were. The man reached the arm of his shabby, black coat around her and explained to his daughter that they were his physics apparatus. Even at such a tender age, the petite girl who would one day become the world-famous Madame Curie was intrigued by science.

She was undoubtedly influenced by her father, a science professor, whose career was stifled by the Russian occupation of Poland. After the bloody Polish uprising of 1863, Russian authorities prohibited him and other Polish professors from teaching physics and chemistry. Years later, Marie Curie wrote that the Russians cheated her father out of what could have been an outstanding career in science. While Professor Sklodowski (Polish surnames are often spelled differently for men and women) continued to read scientific journals and reports, he had no laboratory in which to conduct experiments. Instead, behind locked glass doors, his physics apparatus remained quiet on the dusty shelves. One day, however, his inquisitive daughter would color in the black and white pages of her father's empty dreams.

RUSSIAN OCCUPATION

At one time, Poland had been a proud country. In 1815, with Napoleon's final defeat at Waterloo, however, Tzar Alexander I of Russia was crowned "King of Poland." The devastated country fell under the joint rule of Russia, Prussia, and Austria. The name *Poland* was even erased from many maps, and over the faded patch the words "the Vistula" were written—chosen after a river of the same name. The Russians ruled Poland with a heavy hand and did all they could to erase the Polish culture. Schools were forbidden to teach in the Polish language or teach Polish history and literature. The official language of the land was Russian, and all street and shop signs were written in Cyrillic—the Russian alphabet.

During the Russian occupation, there were two Polish uprisings, both of which failed. The first occurred in November 1830. Wladyslaw's father (Manya's grandfather), Jozef, a respected physics and chemistry professor, fought in the artillery. He was captured by the Russians and forced to march barefoot 140 miles (225 kilometers) to a prison camp. He lost 40 pounds (18 kilograms) during the long, hard trek. By the time he reached the camp, his feet were swollen, torn, and bloody, and they caused him pain for the rest of his life. Jozef made a miraculous escape but sadly did not return home to a free Poland. The Russian Army stomped out the last of the rebellion in October 1831.

More than 30 years later, in January 1863, another rebellion erupted. For a year and a half, Polish rebels fought in vain, some armed only with clubs or garden spades. Thousands of nationalists died in battle or were exiled to Siberia. One of Manya's uncles was injured in the uprising. Another uncle spent four years in Siberia. About 140,000 Polish nationalists packed up as many of their belongings as they could carry and fled to nearby countries; most of the refugees ended up in France. In August 1864, the leaders of the rebellion were captured and hanged. As a reminder

NATIONALISM

Many Poles, like the Sklodowskis, had a strong sense of nationalism. This feeling is inspired by an aspiration, or desire, for independence. Oftentimes, nationalism creates loyalty to an "imagined country," the one that will exist after independence, or when independence is restored to a country that has fallen under foreign rule. Nationalism instills unity among people of a common culture, even when these people have never met one another and maybe never will. From the French Revolution in 1789 to World War II in 1939, many European countries fought to build their own nation-states—Poland among them. Besides the two uprisings, in 1830 and 1863, the Poles again began to agitate against Russian rule in the early 1900s. A series of strikes and demonstrations for civil rights took place, and paramilitary groups formed. Finally, after World War I, Poland gained its independence from Russia.

of what happens to rebels, the Russians left the bodies dangling from the ramparts of the Alexander Citadel, just a few blocks from the Sklodowski home. The corpses remained there for months, slowly rotting in the summer heat.

Manya's family were not only proud Polish nationalists. She also belonged to a family of intellectual scientists. Her grandfather Jozef attended Warsaw University but decided to teach in less-repressed provinces. Wladyslaw was not able to attend Warsaw University because it had been shut down back during the November Uprising of 1830. Instead, for a time, he was forced to take private tutoring in biology until he began classes at the Science University of St. Petersburg in Russia. There, he earned a degree in mathematics and physics, and then took a position as an assistant teacher in Warsaw. His salary was so meager, though, that he could not afford to get married. Luckily, he had fallen in love with a beautiful, exceptionally intelligent woman, who already had a well-established career.

Bronislava Boguska, like Wladyslaw, was from a family in the lower aristocracy known as the Szlachta. This social class had managed to keep some symbols of its status, such as royal crests, and villages that had been named after its families retained those names. Over the years, however, most of these families had lost their wealth and landholdings. Nevertheless, they clung tightly to their love of learning, many becoming priests, doctors, teachers, and musicians. Although 40 percent of the peasant class was actually richer, the Szlachta did not measure their wealth in worldly goods. They felt far more superior because of their intellectual achievements. Bronislava's family was no exception. They scraped together enough money to send her to the Freta Street School, the only private school for girls in Warsaw. Russian officials monitored all private schools. The Freta Street School, however, was not as closely monitored as the boys' schools. Russian officials, like most of society at the time, believed women would never enter into public life, politics, or any other influential position. Most women worked in the home or held jobs in factories and sweatshops, earning a fraction of men's wages.

By the time she had met Wladyslaw, Bronislava had worked her way up from being a teacher to being the head-mistress of the Freta Street School. She brought home a steady income, which included a spacious ground-floor apartment near the school in the center of town. She married Wladyslaw in 1860 and took on both the role of housewife and financial supporter of the family. In the first six years of their marriage, Bronislava and Wladyslaw had five children—Zofia (nicknamed Zosia) in 1862, Josef in 1863, Bronislava (Bronya) in 1865, Helena (Hela) in 1866, and on November 7, 1867, Bronislava gave birth to her last child—Marya Salomee (Manya).

Soon after Marya's birth, Wladyslaw was appointed assistant director of a Russian gymnasium (or school) on Novolipki Street. His new position at this school also offered an apartment, so his family moved to the outskirts of Warsaw. For a while, Bronislava made the long commute to the Freta Street School. But between the long hours and the stressful responsibilities, her health began to suf-fer. Eventually, she resigned from her position at the Freta Street School and became a full-time mother, tutoring Zosia and Josef at home. To save a few rubles, she taught herself to be a cobbler and set up a bench in the house to make her children's shoes.

HER MOTHER'S ILLNESS

In 1871, when Manya was four, her mother developed a persistent cough and began to lose weight—two signs of the deadly lung disease tuberculosis. On the advice of two doctors, Wladyslaw decided to send his wife away for a series of treatments. At the time, doctors believed that

Marie Curie was born in 1867 in this house on Freta Street in Warsaw, Poland. Her mother, Bronislava, was the headmistress of the Freta Street School, and the position included a ground-floor apartment in this building. Today, the apartment houses a museum dedicated to Curie.

tuberculosis could only be cured by a long stay in a mild climate or in the mountains, where the patient could rest and drink curative waters. Although Bronislava hated the idea of being so far away from her children, she reluctantly agreed to go. Unable to afford a nurse, she took 10-year-old Zosia with her. The first cure Bronislava tried was in the

Austrian Alps, near Innsbruck. It was followed by one in Nice, France. By the second year, Bronislava and Zosia had grown quite homesick. On Christmas Eve in Nice, they set the table just as they would have at home—for the whole family. As Bronislava broke a sacred wafer that Wladyslaw had sent from Warsaw, she prayed, "May God make this the last Christmas away from my family."[1]

Back in Warsaw, the rest of the children felt the pangs of being separated from their mother. Wladyslaw took over running the household. Although he did his best to take care of the children, he lacked the gentle hand of a mother. Each hour of the day and evening was scheduled with periods of study and exercise. Manya later recalled that even casual conversations became moral or academic lessons. When the family took a walk in the country, Wladyslaw explained the scientific properties and mysteries of nature. A sunset turned into a lesson on astrological movements. The only time the children got a break from lessons was on Saturday nights from 7:00 to 9:00, when their father would read to them. Professor Sklodowski was not only fluent

DID YOU KNOW?

The Museum of Marya Sklodowska-Curie is the only museum devoted solely to the life of Marie Curie. Established in 1967, the 100th anniversary of Curie's birth, the museum is located in the historic building at 16 Freta Street in Warsaw where Curie was born. The four rooms in the museum show the everyday life and work of Curie as well as her scientific achievements, her honors, and the long-term consequences of her discoveries. The hallways between these rooms are filled with photos and quotations to help understand the social climate and problems of her times.

in his native Polish language, but also in Russian, French, German, and English. On Saturday nights, he would translate classic books, such as *David Copperfield*, into Polish as he read aloud to the children. Manya especially loved *A Tale of Two Cities*, in which a patriot had been reduced to making shoes. This story reminded Manya of her mother—days that seemed so long ago—when she watched Bronislava stitch her tiny shoes. Because Bronislava was a devout Catholic, the children studied the catechism, and every Sunday, an aunt took them to church, where they prayed for their mother's quick return. At bedtime, Manya prayed for her mother to get better.

All of the Sklodowski children excelled in school, but Manya was the most brilliant. One day when she was four years old, she watched her sister Bronya struggle to read a book. As soon as Bronya set the book down, Manya picked it up, flipped open the cover, and read the first sentence flawlessly. When she looked up, she saw her brother and sisters staring at her in amazement. Thinking she had done something wrong, Manya started to cry. "I didn't mean to do it," she sobbed, "but it was so easy."[2]

At first, she and Hela attended the Freta Street School, but after Manya turned six, they transferred to a school closer to their home. There, Manya was placed in third grade, even though most of her classmates were a year or two older. The new school was more closely monitored by the Russian government than the Freta Street School, but it was still run by a Polish Patriot—Madame Jadwiga Sikorska. To deceive the Russian officials, Madame Sikorska wrote two schedules. On the Russian schedule, Botany was written instead of Polish history, and German Studies was actually Polish literature. Madame Sikorska devised a warning system in case a Russian inspector suddenly showed up at the school. As soon as the inspector was spotted, the lookout would ring a bell in a special series. At the warning, students would quickly hide their Polish books and pull out Russian ones.

Manya was a star pupil—praised by teachers for her amazing memory. One day, a friend read her a poem. Manya like it so much, she asked him for a copy. Teasing her, the friend said that he would only read it one more time. If her memory was as good as everyone said it was, she would be able to recite it back by heart. After he read it, Manya sat down and wrote the poem word for word.

Professor Sklodowski instilled in his children a hope of Polish nationalism and a deep hatred of Russia. On the way to school each morning, Manya and a friend walked past a pillar that had been erected by Tzar Alexander II. It read: "To THE POLES FAITHFUL TO THEIR SOVEREIGN." The inscription meant that the Polish people should remember to be loyal to the Russian government. As the two girls walked by, they each spit on it. One day at school, the dreaded bell tolled—rattling rings, two long followed by two short. The children scurried to hide their Polish texts before the inspector walked into the classroom. To test the children, he picked a student and asked the child a question in Russian. The student then had to answer the question in perfect Russian as well. On this day, he picked shy Manya. "And who is our beloved Tzar?" he asked, as recorded in *Obsessive Genius*. Manya replied, "Tzar Alexander II."[3] As soon as the inspector left the room, Manya burst into tears. She hated even the thought of the Tzar. When Alexander II was assassinated by a terrorist bomb in St. Petersburg in 1881, Manya and her Polish classmates danced around the schoolroom.

HARD TIMES

Realizing that open rebellion was useless, Wladyslaw Sklodowski chose to fight for Polish nationalism from the inside. Polish teachers in Russian gymnasiums, like Manya's father, were considered traitors by their countrymen. Wladyslaw, however, felt that he could keep Polish nationalism and culture alive through his teaching. Secretly, he lectured on Polish scientists to give his students pride in their Polish heritage. His patriotic efforts brought hard times to his family, though. The headmaster at the Novolipki Street School was Russian. Before long, he discovered Wladyslaw's clandestine teachings. Immediately, he fired the professor, taking away both the family's income and apartment.

About this time, Bronislava had decided that, no matter how sick she was, she would come home. As soon as Manya laid eyes on her mother and sister, she ran to hug them. She collapsed into Zosia's arms, but when she turned to her mother, Bronislava held out her arm to stop Manya. Although Bronislava longed to hold her little child, she did not want to risk getting Manya sick. Painfully, Manya began to realize that she would never again feel the warmth of her mother's kiss or caress. That Sunday at church, six-year-old Manya prayed that she would give up her own life if only her mother got better. At the moment, she could not fathom just how different events would turn out.

The family now had to rent a house, and Professor Sklodowski opened a boys' boarding school in it to help pay the bills. Before long, 20 schoolboys crammed into the house with the Sklodowski family. Manya had to sleep on the couch in the dining room. In January 1874, one boarder infected Bronya and Zosia with deadly typhus. This disease, transmitted by lice in dirty clothes or bedding, spreads quickly in crowded conditions. During two previous epidemics in Warsaw, thousands of people had died. Suddenly, the house seemed more like an infirmary, between Bronislava's hacking cough and the two girls trembling with fever. After 12 days, Bronya's fever went down, but her sister's did not. Two weeks later, 12-year-old Zosia died. Manya wore her dead sister's long black coat to the cemetery. In shock, she blankly stared at the coffin as she followed it down the street in the funeral procession.

The grief of losing her daughter and dear companion made Bronislava's illness worsen. In May 1878, she died. At church the following Sunday, Manya knelt down to pray as usual, but this time her heart was cold. The death of both her sister and her mother was too much for the 10-year-old girl to understand. She swore she would never again believe in the compassion of God. For weeks, Manya crept alone into deserted places to cry. She hid her sorrow from her family and her classmates. Gradually, she slipped into a deep depression, a shadow that would follow her for the rest of her life. Years later, she would refer to her bouts of depression as "fatigue," "exhaustion," or "nervous troubles," triggered by grief or loss.

Manya's depression never affected her schoolwork negatively, though. In fact, the exact opposite was true. She immersed herself in books for hours, day after day. The only way she could cope with the pain was by obsessively focusing on some subject and completely shutting out the rest of the world. At the end of the 1879 school year, headmistress Madame Sikorska paid a visit to Professor Sklodowski. She told him that she was concerned about Manya. Although Manya was at the top of her class, she seemed abnormally sensitive and emotionally fragile. Madame Sikorska suggested that Manya take a year off of school to heal. Wladyslaw refused to take Madame Sikorska's advice. Instead, he pulled Manya out of the school and Madame Sikorska's nurturing environment. Russian-run gymnasiums were the only schools that led to higher education, so the professor enrolled Manya in Russian Gymnasium Number Three. The education there was excellent, but the Russian teachers worked hard to erase Polish culture from Manya's life. Still, Manya pushed through. At age 15, she

This studio portrait of Manya Sklodowska was taken in 1883, the year she graduated from high school. Manya received a gold medal for her academic achievements. After graduation, though, Manya suffered a nervous collapse. She had been hiding her emotions for years, following the deaths of her mother and sister.

graduated first in her class and achieved a gold medal for being the best student of 1883.

A MAGICAL YEAR

After years of pressure and disguising her feelings, though, Manya suffered a total nervous collapse. She refused to get out of bed and ate little. Instead, she wallowed in a dark room all day. Finally, Wladyslaw became worried about her. He decided to send her to live with relatives in the country. It turned out to be a magnificent decision. She began what would become the happiest, most perfect year of her life. Manya spent the first part of the summer in South Poland at the home of a Boguski uncle. There, she quickly regained her health and good spirits. She put aside her science books and read novels. She fished and picked wild strawberries with her cousins. They took long hikes, rolled hoops, and played games like tag and shuttlecock. Manya drew pictures in a sketchbook—one was of the family dog eating from her dinner plate. At last, she was having the childhood she had never lived.

In July 1884, a former student of Marie's mother invited Manya and her sister Hela to spend the rest of the summer with her family in the foothills of the Carpathians. There, Manya learned to swim and row a boat. The happy house bounced with music—sometimes during the day and sometimes at night. One night, she danced so long that she had to toss her slippers in the trash because there was nothing left of them. She wished that magical time would never come to an end. Back in Warsaw, though, school and her father waited for Manya's return, and that day of reality came all too soon.

Governess

In September 1884, Manya returned to Warsaw. A young woman of 16, she had to set her childhood aside, along with her childhood nickname, and become Marie. By this time, her family had moved into a smaller, cheaper apartment on Novolipki Street. After 30 years of teaching, Professor Sklodowski prepared for retirement. He would collect a small pension, but it was not enough to support his children. Josef ran an ad in a local paper, advertising himself and Marie as tutors. Marie offered lessons in arithmetic, geometry, and French. The job turned out to be frustrating and unrewarding. Marie made long treks across town in the bitter cold to teach students who were either stubborn or lazy. After a year of putting up with undisciplined pupils, she decided to leave home.

Marie took a job as a governess in a lawyer's home. In her naïvete, she expected to love the family, hoping to find pleasant, well-behaved children and understanding parents. Instead, she found the family dreadfully rude and the wife icy and unfeeling. In a letter to a cousin, from *The Curies: A Biography of the Most Controversial Family in Science*, Marie wrote:

> I shouldn't like my worst enemy to live in such a hell. . . . It was one of those rich houses where they speak French when there is company—a chimney-sweeper's kind of French—where they don't pay their bills for six months, and fling money out of the windows even though they economize pettily on oil for the lamps. . . . And, although they speak in most sugary tones, slander and scandal rage through their talk. . . . I learned to know the human race a little better by being there. I learned that the characters described in novels really do exist.[1]

Meanwhile, Marie's sister Bronya was having troubles of her own. Because women were barred from attending the Russian-controlled colleges in Poland, she wanted to study medicine in Paris. She managed to scrape up enough money for the tuition and the trip. Once in Paris, however, she had nothing left for food or rent—even in the inexpensive part of town called the Latin Quarter. Marie—also wanting to study in Paris and unable to stomach the lawyer's house a minute longer—devised a plan in which they could both study in Paris, one at a time. Marie accepted another good-paying governess position at an estate about 62 miles (100 kilometers) north of Warsaw. She would support Bronya while she went to school. Then, after Bronya graduated and became a doctor, Bronya would do the same for Marie.

At the railroad station, Marie took a long, hard look at her father. He was getting old. She worried that she would never

Marie *(left)* and her sister Bronya came up with a plan that would allow them both to study in Paris. First, Marie would work as a governess to help Bronya pay for the expenses to study at the Sorbonne. When Bronya completed her degree, she would then be able to help out Marie. Here, the two are shown in a photograph from 1886.

see him again. They said their good-byes, and Marie boarded the train for a three-hour journey, followed by a five-hour sleigh ride to the home of her new employer—Mr. Zorawski, who managed the estate and farmlands of Princess Czartoryski. It was one of the loneliest days of her life. With tear-filled eyes, she stared out the train-car window, watching the ice-encrusted landscape roll by. When Marie finally arrived at the estate, Madame Zorawski invited her in from the frigid night air and offered her some hot tea. A little later, the madame led Marie upstairs to the big, quiet bedroom where she would be staying. At once, Marie knew that this job would be much better than her last governess position.

SETTLING IN

The oldest daughter, Bronka, was about Marie's age. The two young ladies quickly became close friends. After lessons, Bronka, Marie, and Bronka's 10-year-old sister, Andzia, took walks in the countryside. On chilly afternoons, they went skating on a nearby frozen river. Marie also cared for two other children—three-year-old Stas and six-month-old Martyshna. While she was there, she paid close attention to the agricultural methods used at the estate, which were considered models for the region. She learned all the details of farm work—how the crops, mostly sugar beets, were planted in the fields, the best ways to make the tender plants thick and plump, how to care for the horses in the stables. All winter, the wide plains were covered with snow, and the family would go for long sleigh rides. The driver often liked to tease Marie by moving fast. "Look out for the ditch!" Marie would cry out. "Never fear!" he called back as they went right over it.[2]

Most evenings, she buried her nose in literature and sociology books. After a while, though, she decided that, if she was ever able to study in Paris, she would focus on mathematics and physics.

After only a month, though, Marie began to have mixed feelings about her new job. Although she liked the Zorawski family, she thought Andzia was rowdy and spoiled. Aside from Bronka, she found the local young people boring and uneducated. As time went on, her free time dwindled. She spent seven hours a day tutoring the children. While she found Mr. Zorawski charming, his wife, she claimed, had a hot temper. Marie missed intelligent conversations. Most of the women her age were more interested in gossip than in science. Soon, however, she had an opportunity to put her education to good use. One day in the nearby village of Szczuki, she ended up talking with some illiterate peasant children. They told Marie how much they wished they could read and write. Marie asked Madame Zorawski for permission to use her room to teach these children history and the Polish language. Much to Marie's surprise, Madame Zorawski not only agreed, but she also offered to help, even after Marie warned her that if they got caught they could be sent to Siberia. Marie transformed her bedroom into a small schoolroom with a pine table and chairs. She raided her savings to buy copybooks and pens.

On the first day of class, 10 students showed up for school. Marie taught them for two hours each day, with Bronka and her mother helping keep order. By the end of the year, the class had grown to 18 pupils, and the school day sometimes lasted five hours. Being a schoolteacher turned out to be less rewarding than Marie had hoped. She wondered if the children were already too old to get a full education. She became frustrated, believing she was unable to unlock all of the hidden talents and potential of her students.

DASHED LOVE

About this time, Marie had another new experience developing in her life. She had fallen in love with the Zorawskis' slim, fair-haired eldest son, Casimir. The two met while he was home for a vacation from his mathematical studies at Warsaw University. He was an attractive, intelligent, and spirited 19-year-old and difficult for Marie to resist. Much to Marie's delight, he found her equally charming and asked her to marry him. Naturally, Marie expected the Zorawskis to be happy about the news. After all, Bronka adored her, Mr. Zorawski liked her, and Madame Zorawski had actually grown quite fond of her. But when Casimir asked for his parents' approval to marry Marie, both mother and father flew into hysterics. There was no way their son would marry a poor working woman. Although Marie was brilliant, had an excellent reputation, and was from an honorable family, the social barriers instantly went up. The fact remained: "One does not marry a governess."[3]

Unfortunately for Marie, Casimir did not fight for the woman he loved. Heartbroken and humiliated, Marie wanted to leave immediately. She refused, however, to break the promise she had made to Bronya. So, she stayed on as the family's governess, trying hard to mask her bitter resentment. In the spring of 1888, she still had another year left on her contract with the Zorawskis. She hated every minute of it and gradually became withdrawn, disheartened, and moody. She brooded over Casimir and his parents' ridiculous social expectations. In a letter to Josef, her brother, from *Marie Curie: A Life* by Susan Quinn, Marie wrote, "If [men] don't want to marry poor young girls, then let them go to the devil!"[4]

In the spring of 1889, Marie received some much-needed good news from her father. Wladyslaw had never forgiven himself for depriving his children of the money they needed. Trying to make up for it, he took a job as a director of a reform school near Warsaw. The high-paying position left him enough money to help Bronya with school. For the first time, Marie was able to save for her future life in France. Her attitude suddenly perked up. She left the Zorawskis for a new job as a governess for the Fuchs family in Zoppot on the Baltic coast. Her head was "so full of plans," she told a friend, according to *The Curies*, "that it seemed aflame."[5]

The elegant Mrs. Fuchs immediately fell in love with Marie. She took one look at Marie and called her "exquisite," insisting that she come along to all of their tea parties and dances. After working for the Fuchs for less than a year, Marie received some exciting news from her sister. Bronya and her fiancé, Casimir Dluski, would soon graduate—both as doctors. The couple would then be married. If Marie could save a few hundred rubles to pay for her fees at the Sorbonne, she could live with them for free.

For a moment, the news sunk in like a dream come true. The visions of Marie's Paris education were quickly shattered by reality. By this time, she had already promised to live with her 58-year-old father. A sudden move to Paris might break her father's heart. Marie just could not risk hurting him. She wanted to give him some happiness in his later years. At the same time, it tore her heart to ribbons to postpone college. In the end, though, her family obligations won out. Her pitiful mood was short-lived, as she mapped out her plans to get to Paris one day. She decided that, after she finished her job with the Fuchs, she would live with her father for a year. During this time, she would save up enough money for her Sorbonne studies by giving private lessons. Then, the following year, she would leave for Paris.

During the year in Warsaw with her father, Marie had the chance to work in a chemistry laboratory at 66 Krakovsky Boulevard where her cousin Jozef Boguski was the director of "the Museum of Industry and Agriculture." In reality, however, the museum was just a cover for a so-called Floating University where Poles—both men and women—secretly studied despite Russian bans. There, on free evenings and Sundays, Marie conducted physics and chemistry experiments. The opportunity was like a thrilling adventure. Those evenings at the lab, where glass tubes and jutting arms of instruments cast shadows on the table, were the first sparks of the awakening scientist within. It was no use trying to contain her. On a cold November morning in 1891, Marie again found herself standing on the railroad platform in Warsaw. Once more, she said goodbye to her father and boarded the train. This time, though, there were no tears on the 40-hour, 1,200-mile (1,930-kilometer) steam-engine ride that led to Paris.

PARIS

Bronya and her husband, Casimir Dluski, met Marie at the Gare du Nord station and took her to their nearby second-floor apartment on rue D'Allemagne. It was a working-class neighborhood, occupied mostly by factory and slaughterhouse workers. Marie wasted no time in beginning her studies. In November 1891, Marie took a horse-drawn cart to the Sorbonne's Faculty of Sciences. She was one of only 23 women out of 1,825 students. Despite all of her independent studying, she was not as prepared for college as she had anticipated. As it turned out, her French—which she thought was flawless—was not much better than the "chimney-sweeper's" French spoken at the lawyer's house where she had first worked as a governess. She had trouble following the lectures of the fast-talking French professors. Also, the physics and mathematics she had studied alone or with her father was hardly up to the standards of her French classmates.

Eager to catch up with her classmates, Marie was determined to study as much as possible. Shortly after Marie's arrival, however, Bronya took a trip to Warsaw to visit their father. Marie was left behind to pick up Bronya's household duties. More concerned with her studies than housekeeping, Marie must have made a poor replacement. In a heated letter to Wladyslaw, Casimir complained about Marie's independence and said she showed him no respect or obedience. When Bronya finally returned, the situation cooled

THE SORBONNE

Located in the Latin Quarter of Paris, the Sorbonne is one of Europe's most respected universities. Founded in 1253 by Robert de Sorbon, chaplain for King Louis IX, the college was originally intended for theology students. Students endured a rigorous class schedule, including dialectics, astronomy, grammar, rhetoric, and math. Most days, scholars studied from early morning into late evening. All that is left of the old college are traces of its chapel, visible in the Sorbonne courtyard.

In August 1622, Cardinal Richelieu was elected president of the Sorbonne and ordered the college completely rebuilt. The first stone for the new university was laid on March 28, 1627. In 1635, workers began to build the Sorbonne Church, where Richelieu's tomb was eventually placed. The chapel is the only building still standing from this era. Again in 1883, the university was rebuilt, adding amphitheaters, test rooms, labs, an observatory, and a library with more than two million works—all to accommodate the growing needs of its students.

The college is a huge part of Paris's history. In fact, the Latin Quarter got its name from Sorbonne students who used to speak Latin at the cafés and bistros near the school as a symbol of their prized education. The Sorbonne has an international reputation of excellence, producing some of the most famous scholars in history—including Marie Curie.

down. Bronya persuaded Casimir to rent a larger apartment near a park in La Villette, a Parisian suburb. In the new apartment, Marie had a small room of her own at the end of a hall. Casimir, though, still found ways to interrupt Marie's studies, and the apartment was farther away from the Sorbonne. Marie decided to rent a cheap attic room for 25 francs a month on the sixth floor at 3 rue Flatters in the Latin Quarter, with a skylight view of Paris. And the Sorbonne was only a 20-minute walk away.

For the first time in her life, Marie was living alone. Although she felt lonely sometimes, she loved her freedom and independence. To reach her attic room, she had to climb more than 100 wooden steps. In the winter, she toted along a bucket of coal to feed her small stove. When the coal ran out and she could not afford more, she studied at a nearby library until it closed at 10:00 at night. She then climbed the stairs to her room and crawled into bed, heaping mounds of clothes on top of her to keep warm. Often, she would awaken the next morning to find the water in the washbasin frozen solid. She had to live on just a few francs a day. A typical meal was a cup of hot chocolate or tea heated over a saucer-size alcohol lamp and a slice of buttered bread. On occasion, she had eggs or fruit for a special treat.

Marie was not the only one living on a meager budget. Hundreds of her fellow students shared the same story. She became friends with a group of politically aware Polish students. They would meet in one another's rooms or go on walks together. For long hours, they would discuss their country's enslavement to the Russians and what they could do about it. Although she found the meetings fascinating, her studies took up more and more of her time. So she restricted herself to mingling only with fellow science students. She and her friends marveled at their extraordinary teachers, several of them world famous, like physicist Gabriel Lippmann, who would win a Nobel Prize in 1908;

In 1891, Marie traveled from Warsaw to Paris to study at the Sorbonne. At first, she stayed with her sister Bronya and Bronya's husband, Casimir. Later, she rented a room on the sixth floor of a building much closer to the Sorbonne. Consumed by her studies, she ate and slept little.

Henri Poincaré, one of the greatest mathematicians of his time; and Paul Painlevé, a mathematics professor who went on to become France's prime minister—twice.

In July, Marie took a quick trip home to Warsaw to visit her family. When she returned, she started to have dizzy spells and fainted several times. Undoubtedly, her near-starvation diet was to blame, but she never suspected it. One day, when Marie was playing with her newborn niece, Hela, Casimir told Marie that she looked exhausted. But Marie ignored him. A few evenings later, she fainted in front of a friend, who hurried over to Bronya and Casimir's apartment to tell them what had happened. Casimir rushed to Marie's attic room to make sure she was all right. She was at her desk, studying intently. After rummaging around a bit, he was shocked to find that the only "food" in the room was a packet of tea. Marie admitted that all she had eaten since the previous evening was a pound of cherries and a few radishes. On a nearly empty stomach, she had studied until 3:00 in the morning and slept for only four hours before walking to the Sorbonne.

Casimir ordered her to pack up whatever she needed for the following week's studies and insisted she come home with him. When they got to the apartment, he told Bronya about Marie's meager diet. That evening, they watched Marie finish a meal of rare steak and fried potatoes. That night, Marie slept in her old room, and Bronya made her go to bed at 11:00. For the next several days and nights, Bronya and Casimir supervised her meals and sleep. Marie made a quick and amazing recovery. She looked so healthy and lively that Bronya let her move back to her attic room, as long as she promised to take care of herself. The next day, however, Marie fell back into her old eating and sleeping habits. She was just too focused on her studies to notice when she was tired or hungry. "All my mind was centered on my studies," she wrote, as cited in *Obsessive Genius*. "In the evening I worked in my room, sometimes very late into the night. All that I saw and learned was a new delight to me. It was like a new world open to me, the world of science which I was at last permitted to know in all liberty."[6]

In reality, however, Marie did not know full liberty yet. At the time, society still considered women the "weaker sex." A popular book of the day was titled *The Physiological Feeble-Mindedness of Woman*. In France, respectable women never ventured out unchaperoned, never went to a restaurant alone, and if alone, never invited a gentleman into their rooms. Marie was either oblivious to or unconcerned with these restrictions. She never let popular opinion affect her or her work. Instead, she defied social norms and perhaps unintentionally began to prove them wrong. In July 1893, she took her final physics exam. If she failed, it meant she might have to return to Warsaw in shame. Several anxious days later, she and 30 other students gathered with their families in the Sorbonne's amphitheater to hear the examiner read off the results in order of highest grade to lowest. The first name he read was Marie Sklodowska. In the Sorbonne's long history, never before had a woman graduated at the top of the physics class. She could hardly wait to share the amazing news with her family in Poland. She spent the summer with them in Warsaw. At last able to relax a bit, she once again enjoyed mealtime. Dining with her father and siblings, she traded in her spindly figure for a slightly plump one.

For all scientific professions, mathematics was of vital importance. By fall, Marie was eager to return to the Sorbonne for a master's degree in math. She had emptied her savings, however, and Wladyslaw had nothing left to give her. Bronya, now raising a young child, could no longer afford to support Marie, either. Disheartened, Marie believed that there was no way she would be traveling back to Paris. Then, she received some miraculous news. She had been selected by the Alexandrovitch Scholarship Fund committee to receive a 600-ruble scholarship to study in France. The scholarship was plenty to support her in Paris until she earned a math degree. (Years later, Marie paid back the scholarship so that another poor Polish student could have the same opportunity—something no previous recipient had ever done.)

By September 1893, Marie was back in Paris, living in another sixth-floor room. This time, though, the apartment was in a better neighborhood and was much nicer, with a wood floor instead of cold tile and less-drafty windows. Although it was hard for her to leave her father again, she could see that he was doing well. Besides, Josef was there to take care of him. In a letter to her brother, she wrote, "As for me, it is my whole life that is at stake. It seemed to me, therefore, that I could stay on here without having remorse on my conscience."[7]

Shortly after resuming her studies, the Society for the Encouragement of National Industries hired Marie to test the magnetic properties of various steels. The Sorbonne's crowded physics lab, however, had little room for the proper test equipment. A friend, Professor Joseph Kowalski, who had known Marie since her governess days, invited her to meet someone who had invented a number of delicate instruments that might help her with her work. His name was Pierre Curie.

Setting the Stage

When Marie arrived at Joseph Kowalski's apartment, she had her first encounter with the esteemed physicist Pierre Curie. At 35, Pierre had already made some outstanding contributions to science. He and his brother Jacques had perfected a state-of-the-art quadrant electrometer. This instrument, used for measuring an electrical charge, got its name from the horizontal plates that were split into four sections, or quadrants. An industrial firm called the Central Society for Chemical Products sold them. Shortly before he met Marie, Pierre had formulated a general principle of symmetry known as Curie's Law. The principle stated that "the coefficient of magnetization of a body feebly magnetized varies in inverse ratio to the absolute temperature."[1] This law, which is still used today, began to take shape in Pierre's childhood, when he became interested in crystals and their electrical properties.

That evening at Professor Kowalski's apartment, Pierre was intrigued by Marie as she entered the room. Her ash-blond hair was pinned back, accentuating her simple, delicate features. Pierre could not help but notice her acid-stained fingers—how pleasantly unusual it was at the time to meet a beautiful woman who worked in a lab. Marie was equally struck with Pierre. He stood across the room, framed by a tall French window—a slender man with auburn hair and penetrating eyes. She later described his eyes as those of a "dreamer absorbed in his reflections."[2] Skipping small talk, their conversation immediately delved into the fascinating world of crystals. Marie interjected with intelligent questions. Never before had Pierre talked about his work with a young woman who understood the technical terms and complicated formulas. In those days, women were rare in the world of physics, and stunningly attractive ones were almost unheard of—except, of course, for Marie. The evening was an intellectual feast, with the conversation also touching on social and humanitarian topics. Pierre's slow speech and calm tone put Marie at total ease. By the time the night ended, both Pierre and Marie knew they must see each other again.

They met again at the French Society of Physics and once at his makeshift laboratory. During one of their talks, Marie confided in him how she believed it was her patriotic duty to return to Poland as a teacher and join the struggle for Polish independence. After taking her final exam, she planned to go home to Warsaw. Pierre panicked at the thought of Marie leaving permanently. For 15 years, he had practically avoided women altogether. Finally, he had met someone who shared his love of science. He resolved to see her as much as he could before she graduated. So, he made many trips to 11 rue des Feuillantines in the Latin Quarter and climbed the six flights of stairs to her attic apartment. Like Marie, Pierre ignored social conventions and had no qualms about visiting her alone in her room. It bothered him, though, to see Marie living in such squalor. But Marie did not seem to mind her humble quarters. She cherished the opportunity to continue her studies—no matter if it meant she had to live on very little.

Throughout the spring and summer, Marie got to know Pierre better. He was reserved and sometimes absentminded and an idealistic dreamer. Although undeniably brilliant, he lacked motivation. With Marie's encouragement, though, he developed a thesis titled "The Magnetic Properties of Bodies at Diverse Temperatures." His superb analysis involved working with extreme heat to measure tiny differences in magnetism. He found that heat had little effect on substances that had no magnetic properties. Those that did, however, exhibited a remarkable change of properties at a particular temperature. And the change differed with various materials. Today, scientists still refer to the temperature at which these changes take place as "Curie temperature." Despite his discoveries, though, Pierre was almost unknown in France. At the same time, he was highly respected by his fellow scientists.

FIGHTING FOR HER LOVE

The more time Pierre spent with Marie, the deeper in love he fell. Yet he was completely unaware of Marie's resentment of men following her rejection by Casimir Zorawski and his family. She firmly believed that marriage would stifle her scientific work, and she fiercely clung to her independence. When Pierre finally proposed, she turned him down, claiming that it would be mean of her to leave her father and betray her country. Pierre, though, was determined to marry her. He argued just the opposite—if she moved to Poland, she would be abandoning science.

PIEZOELECTRICITY: A CURIE-BROTHER PHENOMENON

Another of Pierre Curie's contributions to science was made when he was a young man. It developed from his early interest in crystals. Pierre's brother, Jacques, had a professor, Charles Friedel, who had observed that asymmetric crystals—crystals with differing tips—create a polar electricity known as pyroelectricity when they are exposed to different temperatures on opposite ends. In 1880, 21-year-old Pierre and his brother, who was three years older, discovered something new about crystals. As quoted in *Obsessive Genius*, Pierre wrote, "While stretching [similar crystals], we observe the same phenomenon as pyroelectricity but the charges are reversed. The amount of free electricity is proportional to the change in pressure. We have decided to call this phenomenon piezoelectricity."* Then, the Curie brothers carefully cut the edges of a quartz crystal into two parallel sides and covered the crystal with two sheets of tin linked to their electrometer. The charge deformed the crystal. Using this method, Pierre and Jacques discovered that the amount of electrical charge generated by a piezoelectric quartz provided a precise way to balance the weak currents emitted by the electrometer.

At the time, the importance of the Curies' discovery of piezoelectricity was unrealized. The method, however, led to many scientific advances that people today take for granted, such as sonar, ultrasound, cell phones, television tubes, and electrical appliances. For example, quartz wristwatches run off continuous electrical voltages applied to the crystal by a battery. This charge creates piezoelectric pressure, which causes the quartz to vibrate and the watch to keep time.

---

*Barbara Goldsmith, *Obsessive Genius: The Inner World of Marie Curie*, New York: Atlas Books, W.W. Norton & Company, 2005, p. 55.

Perhaps secretly Pierre felt that Marie would be abandoning him, but his words pricked her conscience. Her love for science was strong, and she truly believed that she could do great works with her gifts. Still, she refused to make a firm commitment. Instead, she said in *The Curies*, "I believe you are right. I should like to come back very much."3

In the summer of 1894, Marie took her exams and graduated with France's brightest young mathematical minds, scoring second-highest in her class. She immediately left for Fribourg, Switzerland, to visit Joseph Kowalski—the physics professor who had introduced her to Pierre. After spending some time with the professor and his family, she joined her father in Warsaw.

When Marie left Paris, Pierre worried that he might not hear from her for at least two months. Instead, he received a letter from her just 10 days after her departure. At once, he replied with his first love letter. In it, Pierre professed his love and devotion for Marie in passionate yet practical words, pleading with Marie's logical nature. A portion of this letter is quoted in *The Curies*. He wrote:

> It would be a fine thing . . . to pass our lives near each other, hypnotized by our dreams; *your* patriotic dream, *our* humanitarian dream, and *our* scientific dream. Of all these dreams the last is, I believe, the only legitimate one. I mean by this that we are powerless to change the social order and even if we were not . . . we should never be sure of not doing more harm than good. . . . From the scientific point of view, on the contrary, we may hope to do something; the ground is solider here, and any discovery that we may make, however small, will remain acquired knowledge.4

When Pierre Curie first proposed to Marie Sklodowska, she turned him down, saying she was needed in Poland. After Pierre offered to move to Poland to be with Marie, she realized how much he loved her. In July 1895, the two scientists were married, and this picture was taken soon after their wedding.

Marie was deeply touched by the way Pierre understood how much science meant to her. Still, she seemed unwilling to leave Poland. Although Pierre loved France, he finally offered to move to Poland so he could be with her. His willingness to leave his family and homeland was the ultimate proof of his love. When the situation seemed hopeless, he did not abandon her as Casimir had done. At last, she had found a man who was unable to live without her, and she agreed to marry him.

On July 26, 1895, Marie and Pierre were married at the town hall in Sceaux, France. After the ceremony, the guests walked to the nearby Curie family home. There, in the quaint, sunlit rose garden, they enjoyed a lunch of turkey and peaches. Only a handful of guests were invited to the simple reception, mostly family members and university friends. The newlyweds' gift to themselves was a pair of bicycles, which they would use on their honeymoon. They took a "wedding tramp"—a long bicycle trip down the coast of Brittany and through the mountains of Auvergne. Before setting out, the couple posed for a quick photograph, which showed Marie's handlebars draped with a bouquet of flowers.

After the honeymoon, they moved into a cramped three-bedroom apartment on the fourth floor of 24 rue de la Glacière. Pierre returned to teaching at the EPCI (Ecole de Physique et de Chimie Industrielles, or School of Industrial Physics and Chemistry) at a salary of 6,000 francs a year. He arranged for Marie to have a small space in the same building to continue her work on measuring and quantifying the magnetism of steel products. Pierre supplied the necessary instruments and offered his vast knowledge of magnetism. In this way, the husband-and-wife team began to lay the groundwork for an unmatchable partnership.

ACCIDENTAL X-RAY

In 1895, a barely known physics professor named Wilhelm Conrad Röntgen was busy investigating cathode rays. Until 1831, there had been three states of matter—solid, liquid, and gas. Then, scientist Michael Faraday discovered a fourth, which he called "radiant matter." He used an airless glass tube and applied an electric current to a negative terminal at one end. A flow of invisible rays charged a positive terminal at the other end. These rays, however, remained unnamed until 1876 when German physicist Eugen Goldstein called them "cathode rays." Today, scientists know that cathode rays are negatively charged particles, or electrons.

One Friday night, Röntgen was working alone as usual in his laboratory in Würzberg, Germany. He set up an experiment in a Crookes tube with an anode and a cathode at each end. (In other words, he used positive and negative electrodes, or conductors, by which electricity could enter or exit the tube.) He then attached a Rühmkorff induction coil, which would supply a controllable amount of electric current. Röntgen used a hand pump as a vacuum to decrease the pressure inside the tube. As he pumped, an electric current was released—a beam that traveled between the anode and the cathode as a faint glowing light. Röntgen wanted to see if any light (cathode) rays were escaping from the tube. He could not tell, however, because of the lighting in the room. So, he pulled down the shades and covered the tube with a black cardboard shield. He then repeated the experiment. This time, he noticed something extraordinary. Earlier in the day, he had used a screen to perform some experiments with barium platinocyanide (a phosphorescent material). He had set the screen on a worktable across the room from where he now stood. In the darkened room, the screen lit up with a shimmering glow.

Röntgen repeated the experiment again. The results were the same. Then, he moved the screen farther away and flipped it over, so that its backside was facing the tube. When he applied the electrical charge, the screen still glowed. Röntgen was intrigued. The laboratory was dark, so there was no way that visible light could be the stimulus. Also, the tube had a shield around it so that the rays could not escape unobserved. Somehow, though, rays had penetrated the shield, traveled through the air, and activated the screen. Röntgen realized that he had accidentally discovered a new kind of ray. He named these mysterious rays "X-rays," X being the symbol for an unknown number in mathematics.

For the next eight weeks, Röntgen worked constantly in secret, barring all visitors from his laboratory. He was engrossed in experiments—hardly taking time to eat or sleep. At one point, he tried to deflect the rays by passing his hand between the tube and the screen. Astonished, he saw a skeletal picture of his hand appear on the screen. Next, he placed wood, tin, paper, rubber, and other materials in the same position. Just as with his hand, the interior structure of the materials reflected onto the screen. He called the reflection a "Röntgenogram," which was later referred to as a "shadowgram." He discovered that plates made of glass glowed more or less intensely depending on how much lead they contained. Today, people know that materials with low electron density, such as aluminum, allow rays to be freely transmitted. In comparison, materials with high concentration of electrons, such as lead, block these rays.

To create a permanent image, Röntgen replaced the screen with a photographic plate. The plates captured clear images of the interior structures. Finally, Röntgen decided to share his discovery. He invited his wife, Bertha, to come to his laboratory. He told her to press her hand on a photographic plate. Then, he aimed X-rays at it for 15 minutes. The plate captured a clear image of the bones in Bertha's hand, with a ring on one finger. On New Year's

Day 1896, Röntgen mailed this shadowgram, along with several others, to a handful of well-known physicists in Germany, England, France, and Austria. Two weeks later, the Viennese newspaper *Die Presse* printed the shadowgram of Bertha's hand. Almost overnight, it became one of the most famous pictures in the world.

Soon, Röntgen's discovery would become a major advancement for the medical field. The X-ray allowed doctors to look inside the human body. For example, X-rays passed through the living tissue but could not penetrate a lead bullet, making it easier to treat bullet wounds. At first, however, the amazing discovery had some negative consequences. The possibilities of an X-ray took the world by storm. Instead of heralding scientific achievement, the public turned it into a circus-like sensation. In cartoons, husbands spied on their wives by X-raying locked doors and theater spectators peered through X-ray opera glasses to view naked bodies under the costumes. Because of such cartoons, one New Jersey legislator moved to ban X-rays, claiming they could cause obscene behavior. The public's reaction appalled Röntgen. His important discovery was overshadowed by his newfound fame, which ultimately interfered with his work.

In 1901, Röntgen was awarded the inaugural Nobel Prize in Physics. At the ceremony, the speaker who presented him with the prize stated, "The actual constitution of this radiation of energy is still unknown."[5] This knowledge would not remain secret forever. A few discoveries had to take place first, though.

On January 20, 1896, Antoine-Henri Becquerel, a member of the French Academy of Sciences, attended a lecture on the discovery of X-rays. The speaker suggested that there might be a link between X-rays and phosphorescence. Becquerel's father had invented the phosphoroscope, an instrument used to measure and observe the lingering

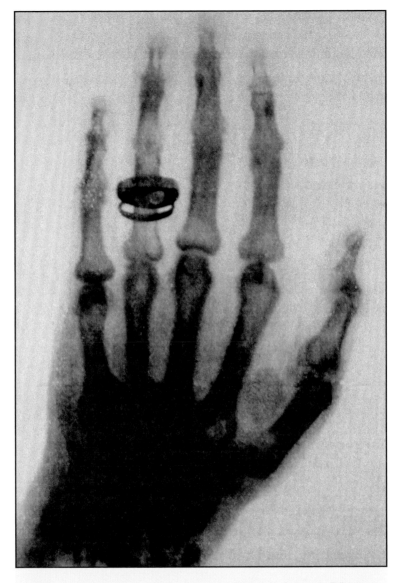

While investigating cathode rays, Wilhelm Conrad Röntgen accidentally discovered a new kind of ray—the X-ray. He found that, by using the rays, he could take images of the interior structures of objects, like this picture of his wife's hand—one of the earliest known X-rays. In 1896, when an Austrian newspaper printed one of the X-rays, the image became famous nearly overnight.

of phosphorescence after the source of light has been removed. After hearing about this link, Becquerel decided to study X-rays.

Within a month, Becquerel had duplicated Röntgen's experiments. Then, he explored substances known to phosphoresce to see if they would also produce X-rays without a vacuum tube and a high-voltage electric charge. First, he placed a sample of phosphorescent uranium salts on a photographic plate of gelatinous silver bromide. He set it on the windowsill to expose it to sunlight for several hours to activate the material. When he developed the plate, a hazy silhouette of the salts became visible. Becquerel concluded that exposure to sunlight had caused the image to appear. Next, he placed a copper cross on the plate with the uranium salts and prepared to expose it to sunlight. Rain clouds, however, covered the sky that February day. Therefore, he wrapped the plate in a black cloth and set it inside a drawer. He would have to wait for a sunny day. Day after day, the rain continued. By March 1, the Paris skies were still gray. Becquerel pulled open the drawer and lifted out the cloth-covered plate. He decided to develop it, even though it had not yet been exposed to sunlight. He expected to see a feeble picture. Much to his surprise, the image of the cross was clearly visible. Obviously, this result had absolutely nothing to do with Röntgen's X-rays.

Becquerel thought these penetrating rays, which seemed to occur spontaneously, might be related to phosphorescence and perhaps held a lifespan much longer than that of X-rays. At once, he informed the Academy of Sciences of his discovery. In 1897, he published six papers on "Becquerel rays." After that, he believed he had done all he could on the subject and abandoned his research. Some scientists criticized Becquerel's work, pointing out that a scientist who worked with Becquerel's father had made the same discoveries and that they had amounted to nothing. Regardless, it was apparent that Becquerel rays displayed neither the clarity nor the dramatic content of X-rays. Few scientists found it worthwhile to pursue this field any further. However, a few scientists did.

A Year of
Great Discoveries

Meanwhile, Marie and Pierre Curie were absorbed in their work. Of course, they had heard about Wilhelm Conrad Röntgen's X-ray discovery. More than 65 percent of the papers read at the Academy of Sciences had been dedicated to the subject. Marie was balancing a hectic schedule between work and domestic duties. She managed to juggle all of her responsibilities until she became pregnant. During the pregnancy, she was nauseous from morning to night. At age 29, Marie was older than most women at the time when they had their first child. Oddly, though, although she felt miserable, her friends said she had never looked healthier.

On September 12, 1897, Pierre's father—a doctor—delivered a six-pound, six-ounce baby girl. Marie and Pierre named her Irène. Now, Marie added caring for a finicky baby to her already overbooked routine. Yet, she was an attentive mother. She started a journal in which she documented Irène's growth and development, almost as if the child was one of her scientific projects. She kept careful records of Irène's head size, when she first rolled over, details of her nursing habits, and the baby's ability to grasp objects.

Although delighted by motherhood, Marie struggled to balance her heavy workload with motherly duties. At lunchtime and in the evening, she rushed home to nurse Irène. Eventually, Marie had to hire a wet nurse, a woman who helped breastfeed a baby. Being unable to feed her own child made her feel like a failure. She fell back into her old eating and sleeping habits, quickly growing exhausted and depressed. She even started to have panic attacks. Suddenly, she would bolt from the laboratory and rush to the park, thinking the nurse had lost her baby. Marie was so distraught and confused that doctors advised her to seek help in a sanitarium, but she refused to leave her husband and daughter. Just as Marie was nearing a nervous collapse, Pierre's father came to the rescue. The same month that Irène was born, Pierre's mother had died of breast cancer. Doctor Curie offered to move in with Pierre and Marie and look after the baby and the house. The family moved to a two-story house at 108 Boulevard Kellerman, on the southern outskirts of Paris. Before long, Marie's health returned to normal.

A RESEARCH CHALLENGE

Back in good health, Marie was finally ready to begin her doctoral thesis. Like many scientists at the time, she was intrigued by Röntgen's X-rays. But Pierre suggested a different topic—the abandoned Becquerel rays. In the final stages of his research, Becquerel had used Pierre's

Marie and Pierre Curie spend a few moments in the garden of their home in Paris with their young daughter, Irène. For a time after Irène's birth in 1897, Marie struggled to balance her enormous workload with new motherhood. The family was helped when Pierre's father decided to move in with them to look after Irène and their home.

electrometer at the EPCI. However, he was unable to master the delicate device. Until this point, only a few other scientists had studied these uranic rays—extremely energetic rays from uranium or other minerals. Anyone who had worked with them found them impossible to measure. Marie decided that she was up to the challenge.

Pierre persuaded his boss to let Marie use a small, damp shop in the engineering school at the EPCI. In December 1897, she set up her laboratory and got to work.

At first, her results were no better than those of her predecessors. Then, Pierre stepped in to help. He worked intensely for 15 days, modifying the electrometer to make it more sensitive to weak currents. He also added a piezoelectric quartz to Marie's list of equipment. This asymmetrical crystal, when it was compressed, measured small amounts of electricity as well as electric currents of low intensity. This piece was crucial in their research, because they used the crystal as the device of electric transfer. Finally, Pierre stabilized the system. Under Pierre's guidance, Marie spent 20 days learning how to use his equipment to measure tiny currents generated by Becquerel rays. Without her husband's equipment and instruction, this feat would have been impossible.

Finally, after 35 days, Marie could begin her experiments. She carefully spread a thin layer of a substance containing pulverized uranium on the lower of two metal plates that she had connected to Pierre's quadrant electrometer. This action kicked off a series of reactions. Uranium rays surging the air between the plates caused electrical changes, more specifically ionization, or the release of electrons from the air molecules. This event allowed a current to flow from one plate to the other. The electrical charges also traveled through a wire to the electrometer. Inside this device, Pierre had suspended a thin, light blade of aluminum, known as a needle, from a platinum conductive wire. A small mirror was positioned farther down the wire. The electrical charge caused the needle to swing slightly, causing the mirror to rotate with it. By bouncing a ray, or beam, of light on the mirror and watching it move along on a graduated scale, Marie could begin to measure extremely weak currents.

Operating the instrument took incredible patience, steadiness, and dexterity, all of which Marie luckily possessed. Years later, her granddaughter commented that Marie was among the few scientists who could blow glass to such a precise thickness that her tubes never shattered under heat and pressure. With rare skill, Marie sat in front of her equipment, intense hour after intense hour, day after day, taking a break only when her back got too stiff. The process she used was extremely tedious. Near her right hand sat a piezoelectric quartz that had been stretched and held secure with small weights. After spreading the test substance and charging the electrometer, Marie focused on the spot of light that reflected off the mirror. Then, one by one, she lifted the weights and placed them onto a small scale until the amount of electric charge that registered on the electrometer equaled the opposing electric charge from the quartz. Jacques Curie had once noted that few people were skillful enough to perform this task. The operator, whose eyes were fixed on the spot of light, had to lift the weights almost automatically—without looking away. This was probably the reason why Becquerel was unsuccessful in his experiments. At the same time as all this was going on, Marie held a stopwatch in her left hand with which she measured the intensity of radiation at a given period of time. At last, infinitely small amounts of currents could be measured—or "weighted."

Within two months, Marie had precisely measured the electrical activity generated by rays from numerous elements. On one day alone, she tested 13 elements. None of them, however, produced rays. The next week, she tested several minerals that contained uranium, along with a sample of pure uranium. The pure uranium gave off the strongest rays of all. Therefore, uranium became Marie's standard of measurement.

One day, something unexpected happened. Marie found that thorium—a mineral element discovered in 1828—produced similar energetic rays as uranium and its compounds. She decided that she would need to expand her search. She began to test many other thorium compounds, including pitchblende, a heavy black ore mined in St. Joachimsthal on the border of present-day Germany and the Czech Republic. Uranium had already been extracted from pitchblende, to be used in Bohemian glass and pottery to create luminous glazes. Surprisingly, the pitchblende ore produced rays stronger than uranium, even though the uranium had been removed from the ore. The outcome did not make sense to Marie, so she remeasured. The result was the same. She decided to recheck the other uranium compounds and then pure uranium powder. But the uranium compounds produced the least activity, and even the pure uranium was not as strong as the pitchblende. In fact, its currents were four times as energetic as those of pure uranium.

Marie compared pitchblende with other substances. She tested the mineral aeschynite, which contained thorium. That, too, was more active than thorium alone. Then, she measured the mineral calcite, which also registered a high degree of activity. Because natural calcite was hard to find, Marie combined its known elements, uranium and copper phosphates, to create an artificial calcite. The radiation emitted from the artificial calcite was no greater than the uranium it contained. But the natural calcite specimen was more than three times as active as artificial calcite. Marie came to the conclusion that there must be another element in the minerals—one that was unknown.

Time and time again, Marie verified her results. Often, she would work late into the night, fueled by intense curiosity. She examined all the elements that were then known, in their pure states and in compounds. She borrowed mineral samples from fellow scientists and dipped into a rare collection of minerals from the Museum of Natural History. Not only did she measure the strength of their rays, but she also tested to see if the energy differed when they were in liquid and solid states, or by exposing them to light or heat. According to her research, however, none of these conditions changed the activity of the samples.

In 1869, Russian chemist Dmitri Ivanovich Mendeléev formulated a periodic table that charted all the known elements. Mendeléev believed that there was nothing smaller than the atom. Therefore, his table was based on the mass and other chemical properties rather than on an element's atomic composition. The word *atom* itself means "indivisible." After Mendeléev discovered a pattern, he placed the known elements in order, leaving spaces for the undiscovered ones he was certain existed. In 1897, English physicist J.J. Thomson discovered electrons, which he believed were

MENDELÉEV'S FIRST PERIODIC TABLE

One night, after having written the properties of elements on separate cards, Russian scientist Dmitri Ivanovich Mendeléev made a groundbreaking discovery. While playing a game of solitaire with his cards, he noticed that by arranging the element cards in order of increasing atomic weight, certain types of elements regularly occurred. For example, a reactive non-metal element was directly followed by a very light reactive metal. A less reactive light metal then followed that element. In March 1869, Mendeléev presented his findings to the Russian Chemical Society. Because his system laid the groundwork for the current period system, he is often viewed as the father of the periodic table.

Mendeléev's 1869 Periodic Table					
			Ti = 50	Zr = 90	? = 180.
			V = 51	Nb = 94	Ta = 182.
			Cr = 52	Mo = 96	W = 186.
			Mn = 55	Rh = 104,4	Pt = 197,4.
			Fe = 56	Rn = 104,4	Ir = 198.
		Ni = Co = 59		Pl = 106,6	Os = 199.
H = 1			Cu = 63,4	Ag = 108	Hg = 200.
	Be = 9,4	Mg = 24	Zn = 65,2	Cd = 112	
	B = 11	Al = 27,1	? = 68	Ur = 116	Au = 197?
	C = 12	Si = 28	? = 70	Sn = 118	
	N = 14	P = 31	As = 75	Sb = 122	Bl = 210?
	O = 16	S = 32	Se = 79,4	Te = 128?	
	F = 19	Cl = 35,6	Br = 80	I = 127	
Li = 7 Na = 23		K = 39	Rb = 85,4	Cs = 133	Tl = 204.
		Ca = 40	Sr = 87,6	Ba = 137	Pb = 207.
		? = 45	Ce = 92		
		?Er = 56	La = 94		
		?Yl = 60	Di = 95		
		?In = 75,6	Th = 118?		

© Infobase Publishing

Dmitri Mendeléev is credited with developing the first periodic table of the elements. Trends could be seen when the elements were ordered according to atomic weight. The question marks and blank spaces predict where future elements would appear on the table.

subatomic—or smaller than the atom. Another scientist, Henry G.J. Moseley, discovered that the number of electrons—not mass—determines an element's atomic number.

By March 1898, Marie had proven beyond doubt that several minerals did in fact give off more energetic rays than pure uranium. In April, she wrote a paper on her research that would one day lead to an entirely new method of discovering elements—by measuring their radioactivity. This method led to atomic science. Marie's paper—"Rays Emitted by Compounds of Uranium and of Thorium"— was read at the prestigious Academy of Sciences. (Neither Marie nor Pierre was a member of the French Academy of Sciences, so they were not permitted to read it themselves.) In her paper, she made two revolutionary observations. First, she asserted that radioactivity—a term she coined in the paper—could be measured, therefore providing a way to discover new elements. Second, she stated that radioactivity was an atomic property—or a property of the atom. Therefore, the atom could not be the smallest form of matter, as many scientists still believed

In her paper, as printed in *Obsessive Genius*, she wrote:

It was necessary at this point to find a new term to define this new property of matter manifested by the elements of uranium and thorium. I proposed the word radioactivity.

During the course of my research, I had occasion to examine not only simple compounds, salts and oxides, but also a great number of minerals. Certain ores containing uranium and thorium proved radioactive, but their radioactivity seemed abnormal, for it was much greater than . . . I had been led to expect. This abnormality greatly surprised us. When I had assured myself that it was not due to an error in the experiment, it became necessary to find an explanation. I then made the hypothesis that the ores of uranium and thorium contain in small quantity a substance much more strongly radioactive than either uranium or thorium itself. This substance could not be one of the known elements, because these had already been examined; it must, therefore, be a new chemical element.[1]

DISCOVERING POLONIUM AND RADIUM

Suggesting a new element existed was a daring hypothesis. She confided in her sister Bronya. "The element is there, and I've got to find it," she wrote in a letter. "We are sure!"[2] Pierre was so excited about the possibility of a new element that he abandoned his own research on crystal growth, expecting to return to it one day. He never did. As enthusiastic partners, the Curies began their quest to find the mystery element. At the outset, they thought the product might be in trace amounts as common as one-hundredth of a part of pitchblende ore. Little did they know it would turn out to be much more minuscule—a millionth of a part. They were about to undertake the most grueling and physically demanding task in the history of scientific research.

On June 6, 1898, red-bearded chemist Gustave Bémont joined the team. The Curies needed his expertise to help analyze the pitchblende. Under his instruction, Marie ground the pitchblende into powder, boiled it in acid, and went through the seemingly endless, repetitive task of separating its elements. As the solution cooled, it formed crystals. The lighter elements crystallized first. In this way, she could separate the elements according to their tendency to form crystals at different temperatures. Marie called this separation technique "fractionation." At each stage of separation and purification, she became more convinced that something in pitchblende was more radioactive than uranium. The Curies came to the conclusion that the radioactivity was basically concentrated in two different chemical fractions. One behaved chemically like bismuth, the other like barium. Finally, she removed every element except bismuth. She added hydrogen sulphide to this crystal-like mineral. The chemical reaction produced a solid that she tested for its radioactivity. In her lab book, she noted the results in bold, underlined words: **150 times more active than uranium**. While Pierre was heating a solution of bismuth sulphide, the glass test tube cracked. He noticed a line of thin black powder on part of the glass. When he measured the powder, he found it to be 330 times more active than uranium. The less bismuth in the mixture, the more striking the results.

Marie was certain that they had discovered a new element, but she needed to confirm it. The best way was by the method known as spectroscopy. In spectroscopy, the chemist heated an element until it turned into a glowing gas and then passed a spark of light across the gas, causing it to form rainbow patterns of light, or spectra. No two elements produced the same pattern of light, and eight new elements had been discovered by this method. As it happened, luckily for the Curies, the EPCI had a resident expert in this field, Eugène Demarçay. He was an odd choice for work that demanded good eyesight, because he had lost one eye in a lab explosion. Nevertheless, the Curies trusted his expertise. Demarçay tested Marie's substance, but it was not pure enough to produce a spectrum. Bitterly disappointed, Marie went back to the laboratory and continued her fractionation. Ten days later, she had extracted a substance 400 times as active as uranium alone. Again, Demarçay tested the substance, but he still could not produce a clear spectral line.

As much as Marie wanted her conclusions to be supported by solid proof, she felt as though she could wait no longer. Other scientists were using Marie's same methods in a race to discover the element before she could. Having established a measurable amount of radioactivity, she felt she had enough proof that the element existed. In July, the Curies wrote a paper titled "On a New Radioactive Substance Contained in Pitchblende." Marie

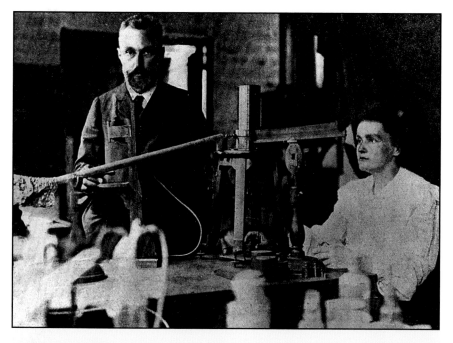

Marie and Pierre Curie are shown in their laboratory in 1898. Marie was finding that certain ores containing uranium or thorium had more radioactivity than pure uranium or thorium. She theorized that these ores included a substance that was a new chemical element.

named the new element "polonium"—after her native Poland. The man who inspired the research—Antoine-Henri Becquerel—read the joint report to the Academy of Sciences. The Academy was impressed with Marie's work on both the magnetic properties of steel and radioactivity. The members awarded her the prestigious Gegner Prize worth 3,800 francs. However, the all-male Academy was too chauvinistic to personally hand her the prize. Instead, members asked Pierre to tell Marie she had won it.

Marie had isolated the element that behaved like bismuth. However, she had yet to uncover a second element that behaved almost exactly like barium. Removing the barium proved a difficult task. Four months later, on a crisp December morning, Marie finally produced a substance whose radioactivity registered 900 times greater than that of pure uranium. Afraid the immense power would quickly disintegrate, she immediately rushed up the stair to Demarçay's laboratory. This time, he found a clear, unique spectral line. On December 19, 1898, Marie made notation of her second discovery—"radium." In only one year, the Curies had discovered two new elements. Years later, the glory of Marie's first discovery—polonium—would fade to almost forgotten. Radium would become her crowning achievement. In truth, however, the real, groundbreaking triumph was her method of discovery—isolating and discovering elements by measuring their radioactivity. Over the following decade, scientists used this method to make more discoveries about the atom and its structure than in all the centuries before. Scientist Frederick Soddy once said, "Pierre Curie's greatest discovery was Marie Sklodowska. Her greatest discovery was . . . radioactivity."[3]

Obsessed with Radium

Marie Curie had discovered two new elements: polonium and radium. Although there was no doubt to their existence, they were not necessarily *proven* to exist. For the most part, physicists were ready to accept the discoveries, because the Curies were working with the properties of rays. Chemists, however, remained skeptical. Until an actual substance could be seen, handled, and weighed, the elements did not technically exist. Marie had to isolate them to prove, without doubt, that a discovery had been made.

During her research, Marie had more success isolating radium. So, she chose to begin there. At the time, she had no idea the magnitude of that task. The same day Marie named radium, she also noted that the new radioactive substance still contained a large portion of barium. Therefore, the radioactivity of the element would get stronger as more barium was removed. Since it was already 900 times more active than uranium, Marie assumed the radioactivity of radium must be enormous, at least several hundred times more active than she had measured. She drastically under-estimated radium, however. In actuality, one tenth of a gram of pure radium was 10 million times more radioactive than uranium alone.

For the first few months, Marie chose to work with small quantities of pitchblende ore residue, not real-izing that the trace amounts of radium in these samples were immeasurable. To produce measurable quantities of radium, she would need a whole lot more pitchblende ore. The Curies had no money to buy the additional ore. So, Pierre went to Eduard Suess, the president of the Academy of Sciences of Vienna, and asked him what typically happened to the pitchblende ore residue after the uranium was removed. As it turned out, the residue was not destroyed. Instead, it was dumped in the forest of St. Joachimsthal. Pierre was able to get Suess to persuade the Austrian government to give the Curies this seemingly worthless material at no charge. Then, Pierre asked Baron Edmond de Rothschild for a donation to cover the cost of transporting the ore to Paris.

The Curies also realized that they would need more work space for such a huge undertaking. They applied to the Sorbonne for lab space in one of its many buildings. Usually, this kind of request was freely granted to sci-entists. For some reason, though, the Sorbonne refused. The director at the EPCI admired the Curies and was sympathetic to their situation, but the EPCI had limited facilities. The best he could offer was a barn-like hangar across the courtyard from their present storeroom labora-tory. The hangar had previously been used for dissecting cadavers, but because of a leaky roof and drafty walls, the corpses had to be moved to another building. Although crude, the hangar offered ample space for storing the large quantities of pitchblende.

When the first shipment of pitchblende arrived, it was dumped in the yard outside the hangar. Marie ran out and scooped up a handful of the brown dust and lifted it to her face. She took a deep, excited breath and hurried inside to begin her work. The first steps in the process were physically rough on Marie's frail body. For weeks, she stirred the boiling residue to make the first reductions; then followed chemical washings, the splitting process, and finally measurements. At times, Marie's goal seemed impossible to achieve, but she refused to give up when many others probably would have. It quickly became obvious to Marie that an infinitesimal amount of radium emitted such strong rays that to isolate the substance itself might take tons of material.

In June 1899, Pierre hired a former student—André Debierne—to help Marie full time. A gifted chemist, Debierne would work as Marie's loyal right hand for the next 35 years. Pierre persuaded the owners of the Central Society for Chemical Products in France to pay Debierne's salary as well as those of several other workers the Curies hired. In exchange, the Curies gave the society a portion of the strong distillates to sell to other eager scientists. The society also agreed to let the Curies use its factory for testing. The factory allowed Marie to take her research to an industrial scale. With Debierne in charge at the factory, a ton of pitchblende was treated in just three and a half months. Each ton of residue required 50 tons of rinsing water. The remaining substance was a bromide 50 times as radioactive as uranium. At this point, Marie took over, taking 20 kilograms (44 pounds) at a time. With Pierre's help, she performed fractionations and measurements, each time ending with stronger and stronger amounts of radium.

By 1901, the Curie team had processed eight tons of pitchblende residue, gone through 400 tons of rinsing water, and performed thousands of chemical treatments and distillations. The substances were arranged on tables and boards throughout the hangar. In the dark, these scraps of radium gave off a faint glow. Marie was enchanted by this "fairy light." She wrote, as quoted in *Obsessive Genius*, "At night . . . from all sides we could see slightly luminous silhouettes, and these gleamings, which seemed suspended in darkness, stirred us with new emotion and enchantment."[1] At the time, the Curies were unaware that prolonged exposure to these substances was damaging their health. Even a century later, their clothes and papers were still radioactive. Pierre was already suffering from rheumatism, which he assumed was caused by the damp air in the hangar. However, his bones were gradually being eaten away by radiation.

In July 1902—the fourth year in her makeshift laboratory—Marie performed yet one more fractionation and measured its radioactivity. Finally, after years of measuring and remeasuring, thousands of fractionations, and 10 tons of pitchblende residue, she had produced a specimen that contained too little barium to influence its atomic weight. She calculated the weight at 225.93, remarkably close to the 226 on today's periodic-table listing for radium. The amount of pure radium was so small, it looked like a few grains of sand—equal to one-fiftieth of a teaspoon. Many people think of radium in terms of beakers and glowing material. Those images actually contain only a minuscule amount of radium. For instance, luminous paint contains just one part pure radium to 35,000 parts zinc. An almost immeasurably tiny amount of radium is incredibly powerful. Using Einstein's equation $E=mc^2$ (energy = mass × the speed of light^2) to calculate the amount of energy in radium, a pound of radium would yield 10 billion kilowatt hours of energy. This energy would be so intense it could provide a year's worth of energy to an enormous power station or, if released all at one time, would equal the blast of a medium-scale atomic bomb. On this warm day in July, however, Marie was thinking only of her scientific achievement. She had isolated radium and properly placed it as number 88 on Mendeléev's chart.

Still, in this time of excitement, Marie's life was also touched with sadness. In Warsaw, Wladyslaw Sklodowski, who had been hit by a tram, was dying. Two months before she publicly announced her accomplishment, she wrote her ailing father and told him about her discovery. Because Professor Sklodowski had always wished to do scientific work, she hoped that news of her scientific triumph would bring him some happiness. In reply, Marie's father wrote, "You are now in possession of pure radium salts. If we consider the amount of work done in obtaining this, it would certainly be the most expensive of chemical elements. What a pity it is that this work has only theoretical interest."[2] His comment, however, could not have been further from the truth. He died shortly after he received her letter. At once, Marie dropped everything and took a train to Warsaw. She arrived just in time for his funeral. Although the coffin was closed, Marie insisted that it be opened. As soon as she laid eyes on her father's expressionless face, she wept hysterically—from grief and the guilt of not getting back in time to say good-bye to him.

TWO DREAMERS

Marie and Pierre Curie were two dreamers obsessed with their passion for science. At night, they would walk the five blocks back to the laboratory hand-in-hand, discussing their research. "I wonder what [the radium] will look like," Marie would say. Pierre, his gaze piercing the dark sky,

Marie and Pierre Curie were obsessed with their work in the laboratory. The couple put science before everything else, rarely stopping to rest or eat. A colleague told Pierre: "It is necessary not to mix scientific preoccupations continually into every instant of your life as you are doing."

could almost imagine it. "I should like it to have a beautiful color," he said.[3]

The husband-and-wife team was almost inseparable. In Marie's mind, she was married to the most wonderful man in the world. She felt that they could read each other's thoughts. Pierre was always there for her, sharing her enthusiasm and shouldering her agonies. One terrible day, suffering from nervous exhaustion, Marie tipped over three months of precious distillates. As the substance puddled on the floor, Pierre took Marie in his arms and comforted her.

Little Irène, however, had to learn at a tender age to share her parents with the demanding work of science. She formed a close bond with her primary caregiver—her Grandpa Curie. At age 3½, she asked him why her mother had to leave her every day for work when most other moms stayed home with their children. Dr. Curie tried to explain that her mother was doing great work. One day, he took Irène to the shabby laboratory. The little girl was unimpressed with the hangar, referring to it as "that sad, sad place."[4] Like most children separated from their parents, Irène longed for her mother's affection. When Marie was home, the child clung to her mother's skirt. When Marie left for the hangar, Irène cried hysterically. At bedtime, she refused to go to sleep without her mother's kiss. Marie, growing up without the affection of her own mother, must have sympathized with her daughter's needs. But she saw herself as a hero on a scientific mission of exploration. It was her duty to perform this research. Still, when Irène was young, the family took a vacation each year to collect some much-needed rest and to give each other some undivided attention.

Friends of the Curies looked at them with concern and slight horror. The couple put their work above everything, including their health. Pierre, who now walked with a painful limp, refused to rest. As in college, Marie was so preoccupied with her discoveries, she seldom ate. Her frail body and pale skin worried all her friends. One friend, also a scientist, cautioned Pierre, "You hardly eat at all, either of you. More than once I have seen Madame Curie nibble two slices of sausage and swallow a cup of tea with it. . . . It is necessary not to mix scientific preoccupations continually into every instant of your life as you are doing. . . . You must not read or talk physics while you eat."[5]

Both Pierre and Marie ignored his advice. Physics pulsed in their veins. For the Curies, it was as necessary as breathing. They believed that nothing worthwhile came without sacrifice. However, it was not painful for either of them. It was a labor of love, a love affair with science that spun its intriguing web around them and never let them go.

THE NOBEL PRIZE

On December 10, 1896, industrialist Alfred Nobel died, leaving behind a fortune from his invention of dynamite. In his will, he designated that his wealth go toward the establishment of annual prizes for outstanding accomplishments in literature, medicine, physics, chemistry, and peace. The first prize in physics was awarded to Wilhelm Conrad Röntgen for the X-ray in 1901. That year and in 1902, Marie and Pierre Curie and Antoine-Henri Becquerel were nominated, but the second year, the prize went to Hendrik Antoon Lorentz and Pieter Zeeman for their research on how magnetism influences radiation. This selection came as a bitter disappointment for Pierre, because he had laid most of the groundwork for these studies.

The following year, in a display of cruel sexism, Marie Curie was left off of the nomination. It was a stunning example of what it was like to be a woman in science at that time. The official nomination for the 1903 Nobel Prize in Physics listed Pierre and Becquerel, but there was no mention of Marie. The scientists who nominated them wrote a distorted account of the discovery of polonium and radium—giving full credit to the two men. Even though Marie Curie's amazing discoveries were known throughout the scientific community, she was not accepted as an equal in the male-dominated field. A friend of the Curies wrote Pierre about the nomination. Pierre responded that, if the nomination was serious, he could not accept the prize

THE MAN BEHIND THE PRIZE

Each year since 1901, the Nobel Prize has been awarded for achievements in physics, chemistry, physiology, medicine, literature and working toward peace. The man behind this innovative international prize was Alfred Nobel. Born in 1833 in Stockholm, Sweden, Nobel was a descendant of Olof Rudbeck, the famous Swedish technical genius of the 1600s. Following in his family's well-known footsteps, Nobel—a chemist and engineer—invented dynamite in 1866. Later, he established dynamite companies and explosive-testing laboratories in more than 20 countries all over the world. Nobel was also a playwright, although this fact is lesser known. His one play of recognition was called *Nemesis*.

In 1888, an obituary printed by mistake called Nobel "a merchant of death." Not wishing to be remembered in such a way, Nobel wrote his last will in 1895, establishing the Nobel Prize. In the will, he stated, as recorded on the Nobel Prize Web site, NobelPrize.org, "The whole of my remaining realizable estate shall be dealt with in the following way: The capital, invested in safe securities by my executors, shall constitute a fund, the interest on which shall be annually distributed in the form of prizes to those who, during the preceding year, shall have conferred the greatest benefit to mankind."* Nobel died of a cerebral hemorrhage on December 10, 1896. Pierre and Marie Curie were the third recipients of the Nobel Prize in Physics.

---

*"Excerpt from the Will of Alfred Nobel," NobelPrize.org. Available online at http://nobelprize.org/nobel/alfred-nobel/biographical/will/index.html.

unless the Nobel committee included Marie. After much debate, the committee finally added Madame Curie's name to the nomination.

And so, Marie Curie received the credit she deserved for throwing open the door to twentieth-century physics. Scientists now had a powerful source of radiation and, for the first time, would be able to witness atomic energy and explore the structure of the atom. Forty years later, physicist Paul Langevin explained how Marie's discovery affected the future. He said, "It may have an importance for the future of civilization comparable to that which allowed man to discover the power of fire."[6]

In November 1903, the Curies and Becquerel received formal notice that they had won the Nobel Prize in Physics. They were invited to Sweden to accept their prize in front of King Oskar II. To the surprise of the scientific community, however, the Curies accepted the prize but declined the trip. They were the first recipients to do so. Although kept secret at the time, the reason the Curies did not go to Sweden was Marie's condition. The previous summer, even though she was five months pregnant, Marie took a bicycle trip with Pierre. After three strenuous weeks of biking, she suffered a miscarriage. When she could throw herself into her work, she was fine. But with the arduous labor of isolating radium behind her, depression crept in. She had not yet had time to finish mourning the loss of her father or her unborn child. For weeks, she laid in bed, barely speaking and eating, ignoring Irène, and leaving the house only to teach classes at Sèvres.

Antoine-Henri Becquerel accepted the prize alone. Again, gender bias became obvious. Marie's name was barely mentioned, except to describe her as a valuable helper to her husband. In fact, the Curies were a team, with Marie, if anyone, in the lead. Nevertheless, 36-year-old Marie Curie became the first woman to receive

The Curies shared the 1903 Nobel Prize in Physics with Antoine-Henri Becquerel *(above)*. In the original nomination for the prize, Marie Curie's name was excluded, an example of the sexism she faced in the mostly man's world of science.

the Nobel Prize. For 32 years, she would remain the only woman Nobel laureate in the sciences, until her daughter Irène Joliot-Curie was awarded the honor in 1935. There was some debate as to whether the 1903 award should be in chemistry or physics because both fields are applied to radioactivity research. For this reason, the Nobel committee left out the discovery of the elements polonium and radium, leaving the opportunity for another award in the area of chemistry.

Lonely Scientist

The Curies were about to find out the price of fame, just as Wilhelm Röntgen had after he discovered the X-ray. In the past, Marie and Pierre had dreamed of a life of solitude—away from other people, engrossed in scientific study. Suddenly, they were bombarded by the press. Only in its third year, the Nobel Prize itself had attracted little attention—especially in the sciences. But Marie Curie had lived the perfect Cinderella story, and the public ate it up. Marie had spent her college years cold and hungry, slaving deep into the night. Then, she met Pierre—her Prince Charming—who whisked her away from her attic dungeon. The love-stricken scientists joined forces in a heroic quest of discovery. After years of miserable toil, they discovered a glowing magical substance that might have the potential to cure the world's worst illnesses. Even at that time, people believed radiation therapy could cure cancer.

Unsurprisingly, Marie handled the sudden fame with calm indifference. After all, she had spent her entire life burying her emotions. On the other hand, Pierre—a very private man—described it as "the disaster of our lives."[1] Although the Curies had actually won the Nobel Prize for discovering radioactivity, the public was fascinated with radium. The Curies were constantly riddled with requests for interviews, hardly experiencing a moment of peace. In Marie's biography of her husband, she included a letter that Pierre had sent to a friend in January 1904. He wrote:

> I have wanted to write to you for a long time; excuse me if I had not done so. The cause is the stupid life which I lead at present. You have seen this sudden infatuation for radium, which has resulted for us in all the advantages of a moment of popularity. We have been pursued by journalists and photographers from all countries of the world; they have gone even so far as to report the conversation between my daughter and her nurse, and to describe the black-and-white cat that lives with us. . . . With such a state of things I feel myself invaded by a kind of stupor.[2]

At the same time, the frenzy also brought with it the long-sought-after rewards for their diligent work. They received the Davy Medal of the Royal Society of London, 12 honorary doctorates, academy memberships in several countries, and highly paid invitations to lecture. After having been rejected by the Academy of Sciences years earlier, Pierre was finally accepted into the prestigious circle. Marie, however, being a woman, was not a member. The fact that these famous scientists were employed in lowly teaching positions became a huge embarrassment for

France. Pressured by public fans and the press, the French Parliament created a new science chair at the Sorbonne with a salary of 10,000 francs and offered the position to Pierre. The position, though, did not include the use of a laboratory. Pierre declined the offer, and the Sorbonne ultimately agreed to grant Pierre a lab, along with three paid assistants of his choice. With a proper lab and Marie as head of research, the Curies hoped that their dream of an ideal life in science had at long last come true. But their daily life was so interrupted by fame, they barely had time to work.

When time allowed, Pierre continued his research on radioactivity. He experimented with the force of gravity on radioactive materials, such as radium and thorium. He also studied the radioactivity of several thermal water sources. Most of his efforts, though, were focused on developing medical uses for radium. Many people mistakenly think that radium treatments for medical ailments immediately followed Marie's discovery. Actually, until the 1930s, these uses were extremely rare because of the scarcity and high price of pure radium.

At first, Marie was only able to produce one grain (0.065 gram) of radium per two tons of pitchblende ore. By 1904, with the help of the Central Society's facilities, she could yield four grains (.26 gram) for each ton of residue. At this time, medical uses for pure radium were still being researched. However, bogus radium treatments flooded the popular market and exploded into a multimillion-dollar industry. Because pure radium was so powerful, it could be diluted up to 600,000 times with substances like zinc sulfide, zinc bromide, or other bromides and still hold its power.

RADIUM 'CURES'

The radium craze stretched over four decades. Products containing radium were believed to cure all sorts of illnesses and were even used for entertainment purposes. Diluted

Our New Radium $5⁰⁰
Home Permanent Wave
Bathing Beauty

COPYRIGHT
1924
H.W. CHERRY

An advertisement from 1924 boasts of a radium hair-styling product. For much of the early twentieth century, products containing radium were sold as cures for illnesses and even as beauty aids. Little attention was paid to the dangers of radium.

solutions of radium were added to tea, health tonics, face creams, lipsticks, bath salts, and costumes that glowed in the dark. Radium elixirs, or beverages, also became popular. The Revigorator—a flask lined with radium—could be filled with water each night to drink the following morning. Radithor, a drink containing one part radium salts to 60,000 parts zinc sulfide, claimed to cure stomach cancer and mental illness and to restore vigor and vitality. An American industrialist, Eben Byers, drank a bottle a day for four years. At the end, he died in excruciating pain from cancer in his jaw as his facial bones disintegrated. Although the Curies warned people about the dangers of radium, many had to find out the hard way. Even the Curies, who had witnessed lab animals die when exposed to radium, did not think that their own deteriorating health was connected to the substance.

The price of radium escalated beyond expectation—validating what Marie's father had said, that it should be worth a fortune. By 1904, a gram of radium cost 750,000 gold francs, or $110,710 in today's U.S. dollars. About this time, the Curies switched their loyalty from the Central Society

IN HER OWN WORDS

The Curies believed that to derive profit from their discovery was against the scientific spirit. Years later, according to *Obsessive Genius*, Marie Curie wrote:

> If our discovery has a commercial future, that is an accident. Radium is going to be of use in treating disease. . . . It seems to me impossible to take advantage of that.

to Armet de Lisle, a businessman who owned a prosperous quinine factory. Their new contract guaranteed the production of radium on a larger scale and a laboratory for research. Although sales from radium had climbed to epic proportions, the Curies were far from rich. They held no patent on radium or the process by which it was manufactured. And they never tried to secure one.

Marie continued her work in the laboratory. For the first time, though, she broadened her once single-minded purpose in life. She was pregnant again and decided that she needed to take care of herself. On December 6, 1904, the Curies' second daughter, Eve Denise, was born.

In April 1905, Pierre and Marie were finally strong enough to make the 40-hour trip to Stockholm, Sweden. Nobel Prize laureates were required to present a lecture, which usually took place at the time of the award. Naturally, Pierre was asked to give the lecture for their 1903 award. Marie could not even sit on the stage with Pierre. The insult, though, was hardly bitter for Marie. From the podium, Pierre gave her full credit for her discoveries. In his speech "Radioactive Substances, Especially Radium," he pointed out that Marie alone had discovered the radioactivity of uranium and thorium. He also stressed that Marie was the one who found traces of polonium and radium in pitchblende ore. For the first time, he also admitted the possible dangers of this discovery. He said:

> It can even be thought that radium could become very dangerous in criminal hands, and here the question can be raised whether mankind benefits from knowing the secrets of Nature. . . . The example of the discoveries of Nobel is characteristic, as powerful explosives have enabled man to do wonderful work. They are also a terrible means of destruction in the hands of great criminals who are leading the

people towards war. I am one of those who believe with Nobel that mankind will derive more good than harm from the new discoveries.[3]

Not all scientists agreed with Pierre, though. Physicist Ernest Rutherford commented that, with all the energy generated by radioactivity, "some fool in a laboratory might blow up the universe unaware."[4]

When the Curies returned from Sweden, they followed their tradition of a summer vacation. They rented a cottage on the Normandy coast, and Marie spent the summer swimming and playing with seven-year-old Iréne and baby Eve. The family returned to Paris in the fall, and Pierre, though exhausted and ill, went back to work. At the de Lisle laboratory, he worked closely with several doctors to further develop potential medical uses for radium.

In April 1906, the family took a short Easter vacation to St. Rémy-les-Chevreuse. On Wednesday, April 18, Marie and the girls returned to Paris, following Pierre, who had left the vacation early to get back to work. Thursday morning, Marie was busy trying to get the girls organized on their first day back at home. When she mentioned to Pierre that she might spend the day with Iréne, he snapped at her. He insisted she come to the laboratory that day. Before he left, he called upstairs to see if she was planning to meet him at the lab. "I don't know," Marie said. "Don't torment me."[5]

Pierre snatched his umbrella from the stand in the front hall and stepped out the door into the pouring Paris rain. He hurried right to the laboratory, then at 10:00, he left to go to a lunch meeting with a group of scientists. After lunch, he shuffled through the puddles forming on the Paris streets on his way to the office to proofread his new paper. When he reached the busy corner of Pont Neuf and rue Dauphine, the street was clogged with traffic—delivery wagons, carriages, cabs, and buses rumbling in every direction. Pierre limped off the street corner, just as a heavily loaded, horse-drawn wagon barreled into the crowded intersection. One horse galloped past Pierre, brushing his shoulder. He reached up to hold onto the horse, trying desperately to steady his weak legs. Suddenly, the horses reared, and Pierre tumbled between them onto the rain-soaked street. The front wheels of the wagon missed him, but the left rear wheel rolled over his head, crushing his skull. At 49, Pierre Curie was dead.

At dusk, Marie and Irène returned from an afternoon at Fontenay-aux-Roses, a nearby suburban village. Apparently, she had ignored Pierre's wishes for her to show up at the laboratory. Paul Appell, the dean of Pierre's department at the Sorbonne, told Marie what had happened. At first, she sat in a long silence, trying to wrap her mind around the words that had just been spoken. Finally, in a whisper so faint it could barely be heard, she spoke, "Pierre is dead? Dead? Absolutely dead?"[6] Years later, Eve Curie wrote about how deeply Pierre's death pierced her mother in her book *Madame Curie*. "From the moment when those three words, 'Pierre is dead,' reached her consciousness, Madame Curie, on that day in April, became not only a widow, but at the same time a pitiful and incurably lonely woman."[7]

"MY CHILDREN . . . CANNOT AWAKEN LIFE IN ME"

Marie refused to have an autopsy done on Pierre's body. Instead, she insisted that his body be brought directly to her. She then walked with slow, heavy steps into the misty garden. There, she sat down on a damp bench, rested her elbows on her knees, and dropped her head into her hands.

The ambulance arrived around 8:00 at night. As soon as the stretcher carrying Pierre entered the house, Marie kissed his face and clung to his lifeless body. Finally, one of the medics had to rip her away so they could prepare

Pierre's body for burial. On the morning of the funeral, Marie placed Pierre's favorite photo of her next to him in the coffin, closed the cover, and sprinkled periwinkles from the garden over the top. Then, she sat alone beside his flower-draped coffin and waited. She wanted Pierre to have a simple funeral and to be buried at Sceaux. But news of his death had spread, and a crowd gathered at the burial site. Marie stood near the gravesite, heavily veiled and leaning on her father-in-law's arm. After the brief service, she dropped more flowers into the grave—one by one. As the crowd finally dispersed, Marie, Dr. Curie, and Pierre's brother, Jacques, said one last good-bye and walked away.

The day after the funeral, Marie went to her neighbors, where Irène had been staying since the accident. Marie had not yet told her eight-year-old daughter the tragic news. Dressed in black from head to toe, Marie was pale and icy. When Marie told Irène that her father was dead, the child continued to play as if she did not hear a word. "She's too young to understand," Marie said and left.[8] But Irène was not too young, and as soon as Marie walked out the door, she burst into tears and asked to go home. Not even two years old, little Eve was the one who was too young to understand. And Marie knew that she would soon forget her father.

Pierre's death marked a dark turning point in Marie's life. She fell into a chronic state of depression, only relieved by immersing herself in work. Never again would happiness brighten her face. Just as after her mother died, Marie hid her sorrow, speaking to no one about the pain she suffered. A couple of weeks after the funeral, Marie flipped open a gray notebook and began to write a diary to Pierre. In most of the entries, Marie wrote to Pierre as if he were still alive, sitting across from her at the supper table or walking beside her on the way to the laboratory. To some, these entries may seem odd and eerie. However, the Curies—especially

Marie Curie posed in a 1908 photograph with her daughters Eve *(left)* and Irène. Marie fell into a chronic depression after the 1906 death of Pierre Curie. The laboratory became the only place she could endure a life without her husband.

Pierre—believed in spiritualism. The basic principle of this belief is that the living can still communicate with the dead. Very few scholars have been allowed to read the private and intimate diary. The tear-splotched entries reveal the complicated and passionate side of Marie's personality.

In the diary, Marie chastises herself for not going to the laboratory with Pierre that final day. Instead, she spent the day with Irène, against her husband's wishes. Her last words to him were sharp. She relived those final ticking minutes day after day, overcome with guilt and pain. "When you left, the last sentence that I spoke to you was not a sentence of love and tenderness," she wrote in her diary. "Nothing has troubled my tranquility more."[9]

After the funeral, instead of letting her family comfort her, Marie immersed herself in work. At the laboratory, she was surrounded by painful reminders of Pierre. But she knew she had to continue their research. It was what Pierre would have wanted. "I want to talk to you in the silence of this laboratory, where I did not think I could live without you," she wrote to him. "I tried to make a measurement for a graph on which each of us had made some points, but . . . I felt the impossibility of going on. . . . The laboratory had an infinite sadness and seemed a desert. It seems at one moment that I feel nothing and that I can work and then the anguish returns."[10] Over the next 10 months, she pushed on through the grief, devoting her time to verifying Pierre's experiments on radioactivity and how its invisible rays transmit through air to nearby substances and objects. She completed Pierre's half-finished book on the force of gravity on radioactive materials, such as radium and thorium. However, she refused to take any credit for this 600-page book. Next, she edited *Works of Pierre Curie*, for which she wrote the introduction.

On May 11, 1906, Marie was asked to take Pierre's place at the Sorbonne. She was the first woman to obtain this type of a position in the history of the university. On November 5, she prepared to give her first lecture at 1:30 in the afternoon. By 10:00 in the morning, hundreds of people lined up in front of the lecture-hall doors. When the doors opened at 1:15, several hundred eager spectators—students, photographers, journalists—pushed their way into the room. Most people probably anticipated that Marie would offer a tearful tribute to her late husband, but if so, they were sadly disappointed. After quietly slipping into the physics hall, she began her lecture in an icy, unemotional voice, picking up at the exact spot where Pierre's final lecture had ended. Despite her matter-of-fact performance, inwardly Marie was drowning in anguish. She later wrote in her diary, "Yesterday I gave the first class replacing my Pierre. What grief and despair! You would have been happy to see me as a professor at the Sorbonne . . . but to do it in your place, my Pierre, could one dream of a thing more cruel. And how I suffered with it, and how depressed am I."[11]

Depression shadowed Marie like a dark veil over her face. She no longer enjoyed the sun or their garden full of flowers. Instead, she preferred days gray and dreary, like the day when Pierre died. She loathed social settings and avoided any situation that was not directly linked to scientific work. The laboratory became her safe harbor, the only place she could endure a life without her beloved Pierre. At home, Iréne and little Eve longed for their mother's soft caress and warm smile. At least Iréne could remember the woman who lived in her mother's body before Pierre's death. Although obsessed with scientific work, Marie still laughed and loved and splashed in the water on their seaside summer vacations. Eve was only 16 months old when Pierre died. She had no memory of an affectionate mother. Years later, when Eve wrote a biography of her mother's life, she chose to title the book *Madame Curie*. Marie Curie, she said, would have been too intimate.

Somewhere inside her heart, Marie wanted to give her children the love they lacked. But there was no love inside her to give. She wrote of her daughters, "They are both good, sweet, and rather pretty. I am making great efforts to give them a solid and healthy development. . . . I want to bring up my children as well as possible, but even they cannot awaken life in me."[12]

A Better World

In a 1910 edition of *Le Temps* newspaper, a well-known scholar wrote the following about Marie Curie: "Madame Curie since the death of her illustrious husband has not accomplished anything by herself. . . . She has stood by the wayside while others are unraveling the mysteries of the atom."[1] The man who made this statement, though, obviously did not understand Marie's work. She was not interested in discovering the structure and hidden power inside the atom, as other scientists were doing. Rather, she and her laboratory were dedicated to medical, biological, and industrial research. In addition, one of Marie's important contributions to science was her persistent and impeccable work in metrology—the science of weights and measurements. Using an approach that combines physics and chemistry, Marie had practically made an art out of measuring radioactive substances. In this field, she was the best in the world.

At that time, radioactivity dealt with the spontaneous emission of radiation from elements like radium, polonium, and thorium, as well as the study of the physical and chemical properties of these elements. Marie remembered her husband's warning that, if radioactive substances fell into criminal hands, they could lead to massive destruction. She hated war, and instead, wanted to develop peaceful uses for radioactivity that could benefit humanity. She pursued the use of radium for medical treatments and for industrial uses. In essence, Madame Curie firmly believed her research could help create a better world.

Once she had finished the work Pierre had started, the lab on the rue Cuvier became her own and mirrored *her* goals. The de Lisle factory processed her materials and manufactured products used for medical and industrial purposes. For Marie's work, she sought to measure what she called "the chemistry of the invisible."[2] She wanted to figure out how to identify a radioactive element and measure its energy if there was no way she could isolate it. André Debierne was Marie's ally in this mission. Debierne negotiated with radium factories, set up facilities, and conferred with other scientists to make sure that Marie dominated the study of radium. After Dr. Curie, Pierre's father, died in 1911, Debierne even cared for her children when Marie had to work late. Marie concentrated not just on radium but also on polonium. With polonium near its final stage, she performed the last fractionations until the element could be verified by spectroscopy. Although the concentration of polonium in pitchblende ore was 4,000 times less than radium, its power was even stronger. The Curie laboratory became the foremost institution dealing with the production and certification of radium. From 1906 to 1910, the number of her employees grew from eight to 42, including 20 female scientists who volunteered to work without pay.

In France, there were two other laboratories that measured the strength and content of radium salts and various radioactive isotopes. Neither one, however, functioned as efficiently or as accurately as the Curie. In 1911, Marie started an authentication service, guaranteeing products from the Curie laboratory as authentic, or genuine. The laboratory issued a numbered certificate to its customers. Throughout the world, other factories were producing various strengths of radium salts. Often, they were much weaker than advertised. Marie's lab, however, was the utmost authority on the metrology of radioactivity. She was the best, and she knew it. Because these substances were so valuable, it was important that there were no errors in the strength of the quantities being sold. The market needed a standard. Marie created one by measuring how much weaker or stronger the radioactivity was compared with pure radium.

Marie hoarded her valuable information. Other laboratories wanted Marie to check their standards against hers, but she refused. When the International Congress of Radiology and Electricity met in Brussels in September 1910, Marie deceitfully told the group that she and Debierne had formulated a precise standard, but she was keeping it hidden in her laboratory to check the gamma radiation level. When the International Radium Standard Committee offered to buy her specimen, she said she wanted to keep it for sentimental reasons. Fellow scientists began to see her as a stubborn and prickly woman.

At a second session, the committee tried to appeal to Marie's vanity. The committee members suggested that the standard unit of measurement be called a *curie* but added that the specimen must be turned over. The standardization process actually ended up taking Marie three years, primarily because she got sidetracked by yet another sexist blow. Once again, she had to prove her abilities as a scientist.

AN ENVIOUS COLLEAGUE

No matter what Marie did, no matter how precise her research was, she could not seem to earn the respect of her male colleagues. Just as she was being wooed on the radium standard, William Thomson—Lord Kelvin—driven by sexism and jealousy, tried to discredit her discovery of radium. At age 82, he wrote a letter to the *London Times* stating that radium was not an element at all, but rather, he claimed, it was a helium compound. As it turned out, Lord Kelvin had a bone to pick with Marie. In 1862, he had become famous for his studies setting the age of the Earth at 20 million to 50 million years. Marie's discovery of radioactivity, followed by her verification of Ernest Rutherford's transmutation theory, put the age of the Earth at twice or more Lord Kelvin's figure. Lord Kelvin's little stunt caused an uproar in the scientific community, especially when several other well-known male physicists agreed with him.

True to character, Marie did not respond with mere words. Instead, she set out to find more scientific evidence of her discovery—no matter how long it would take or how hard the task. First, she performed an even more specific study of the atomic mass of radium. She published a result of 226.45, plus or minus 0.5. (The current atomic weight of radium is 226.025.) Next, with bitter determination, she embarked on a mission to create radium as a pure metal for chemists to see and touch.

Almost as challenging as her original quest for pure radium, the process took her three grueling years. At last, she produced a tiny square of shiny white metal that had a melting point of 700 degrees and that darkened almost immediately when exposed to air. In 1910, she published her study in the two-volume *Treatise on Radioactivity*. She

Despite her many accomplishments, Marie Curie continued to have to combat discrimination from male scientists. One famous physicist— William Thomson, Lord Kelvin—disputed Curie's discovery of radium. So she set about to create radium as a pure metal, to be seen and touched.

had finally put the question to rest once and for all. And yet, her male colleagues, glowing a fluorescent green with jealousy, were not satisfied. Rutherford, while admitting that he wished he had written the book, criticized it by saying that it had too much information.

During these three years, rich sources of radioactive ore had been discovered around the world. The Curie laboratories continued to increase in importance but not in size. On the rue Cuvier, Marie's staff was working in cramped quarters, and the de Lisle factory was overloaded. Austria offered to build a state-of-the-art laboratory for Madame Curie. There was no way, though, that she would leave France. At the same time, the offer turned out to be a bargaining chip for her to begin negotiations with the Pasteur Institute to build a radium institute for her. The new facility would be part of the existing institute and consist of the Curie and Pasteur Pavilions joined by a garden in between. At the height of her career, it looked as though she would finally get the laboratory she and Pierre had desired. But Pierre was dead, and Marie's longing to fill the void was almost her undoing.

THE GREAT SCANDAL

On a warm April evening in 1910, Marie dropped by the house of Émile and Marguerite Borel. Émile Borel was the dean of the École Normale Supérieure, and his wife was the daughter of Paul Appell, dean of the School of Sciences at the Sorbonne. The Borels had invited Marie, along with Jean and Henriette Perrin, for an informal dinner party. Jean Perrin, an expert in cathode rays, was part of the Curie team, and his wife, Henriette, had much affection for Marie. This close-knit group of colleagues was loyal and devoted to Marie. They would soon be called on to prove it as part of what would later be called "the Great Scandal."

On the night of the dinner, Marie appeared almost transformed—as though she had been replaced by a shoddy, yet radiant, imposter. She walked through the door dressed in a fashionable white gown, with a single pink rose pinned at her waist. It was a striking switch from the grim black dress she had worn every day since Pierre's death. The guests at the party were so shocked by the new Marie, that the next morning Jean Perrin asked Marguerite Borel, "What happened to her?"

What happened to her was a man—Paul Langevin, Pierre's former student, who had been a dear friend of the

THE RADIUM INSTITUTE AND THE CURIE MUSEUM

The Radium Institute—specially built for Marie Curie by the University of Paris—was erected just a few streets away from the "shed" where the Curies discovered polonium and radium in 1898. When construction was finished in 1914, the Radium Institute, part of the Curie Pavilion, faced the Pasteur Pavilion, which housed the Pasteur Laboratory as part of the Pasteur Institute. For the next 20 years, Marie feverishly worked in the Curie laboratory, isolating and purifying polonium. The institute became a world center for the study of radioactivity, as well as an international center for measuring the radium content of various products. It was in this institute that her daughter Irène and Irène's husband, Frédéric Joliot, discovered artificial radioactivity, for which they received the Nobel Prize in chemistry in 1935.

As Marie's health and eyesight began to fail, she focused her energy on directing the institute. Seeing that science was becoming more and more specialized, she formed major lab teams devoted to a single subject. Each team tackled specific questions and trained students in their methods. Marie

Curies and became Pierre's successor at the EPCI. Tall and muscular, he had captivated Marie with his piercing gaze, his chic handlebar mustache, and his suave slicked-back haircut. Five years younger than Marie, Langevin was a brilliant mathematician and physicist. In 1906, he had reached the conclusion that E=mc² only to find out that a fellow scientist—Albert Einstein—had already published this same discovery. Naturally, Marie was drawn to his exceptional intelligence. Often, he helped her prepare course lectures for the Sorbonne. Throughout the early years after Pierre's death, he lent a sympathetic ear to

personally kept in touch with the work details of every one of the three to four dozen researchers. She considered her researchers "children," with Irène and Frédéric Joliot the stars of the family. From 1919 until Marie's death in 1934, scientists at the Radium Institute published 483 works, including 31 papers and books by Madame Curie herself.

In 1964, on the thirtieth anniversary of the discovery of artificial radioactivity, display cabinets holding some of the most important research apparatus used until the 1930s were installed at the entrance of the Curie Pavilion. In 1967 (100 years after Marie's birth), researchers began to show her office and personal chemistry lab—still intact—to privileged visitors. Because of the growing number of visitors, in 1981, Marie's lab was decontaminated and reconstructed. By 1992, the Curie Museum on the ground floor of the pavilion had opened to the public. Here, exhibits retrace the history of radioactivity and its applications—notably in medicine. The museum acts as a guardian of the heritage, memories, and history of this great science.

Marie. And before long, he was asking her for advice on what he called a "disastrous mistake of a marriage"[3] to Jeanne Desfosses, the daughter of a working-class ceramic artist. Langevin confided in Marie that he felt suffocated in his marriage, that his wife held him back from making great discoveries.

In time, the friendship grew into affection. By July 1910, they had become secret lovers. In Langevin, Marie saw the potential for another great partnership—mirroring the one she had with Pierre. She felt as if life had handed her a second chance at happiness. Believing that Langevin wished for the same companionship, Marie hoped and even expected he would leave his wife for her. In a letter to him, she wrote, "It would be so good to gain the freedom to see each other as much as our various occupations permit, to work together, to walk or travel together. . . . The instinct which led us to each other was very powerful. . . . What couldn't come out of this feeling?"[4]

Marie was not the first lover Langevin had taken during his marriage. In the past, his wife had somewhat tolerated her husband's affairs. However, she often flew into terrible rages, one time even gashing open his head with a broken bottle. This time, Jeanne Langevin was not so forgiving. She felt genuinely threatened by the famous Madame Curie. One night, she even threatened to kill Marie. Jeanne and her sister crouched in the dark shadows across the street from Marie's apartment. As Marie walked by, Jeanne suddenly stepped out of the night into the yellow glow of a street lamp. She ordered Marie to leave France immediately or die. When Marie confronted Langevin about the incident, he told her that his wife was completely capable of murder and advised her to do as Jeanne said—leave France. Marie refused and instead, began to live like a hunted beast, leery of what might be hiding around every corner. The stress and worry of both the relationship and Langevin's wife weighed heavily on Marie. Her face grew even more worn and tired.

Finally, they decided it would be best to stop seeing each other. But Marie still hoped they would someday be together. The following summer, she and her children went to l'Arcouëst, on the northern coast of Brittany. This resort, a popular vacation spot for scientists and professors, earned the nickname Fort Science. The Borels and the Perrins were vacationing there as well. One night, Marie grabbed Marguerite Borel's hands and poured out her heart. She confessed that she would do anything for Langevin. If she could not be with him, she worried she would sink into despair. In a letter to Langevin, she even went as far as to threaten to kill herself if he did not leave his wife.

Then, she sent several letters, offering ideas on how Langevin could get out of his marriage. She encouraged him to be strong when walking away. "Don't let yourself be touched by a crisis of crying and tears," she warned him. In another letter, she pleaded with him, "When I know that you are with her, my nights are atrocious. I can't sleep. . . . I wake up with a sensation of fever and I can't work. Do what you can and be done with it. . . . We can't go on living in our current state."[5]

Although Langevin seemed to truly love Marie, he had no real intention of leaving his wife. Instead, he continued to drag out the doomed affair, renting an apartment for their secret meetings. Finally, the inevitable happened— they were exposed. Jeanne began to spy on her husband, and in the spring of 1911, she uncovered the hard proof she needed. Buried deep in a desk drawer, she discovered the passionate letters Marie had written to her husband. She threatened to release them to the public. In a rage over the stolen letters, Langevin left home for two weeks but then returned. After another fight in July, he walked out again, and this time Jeanne filed charges of abandonment.

A SECOND NOBEL PRIZE

Worn down with worry, Marie left for Brussels and the 1911 Solvay Conferences. These conferences attracted the greatest scientific minds, including Langevin, Jean Perrin, Albert Einstein, and Ernest Rutherford. During the conference, Marie received a moment of relief from her emotional anxiety. The Nobel committee sent her a thrilling telegram, announcing that she was the sole winner of a second Nobel Prize, this time in chemistry, for producing pure samples of polonium and radium and for her feat of creating radium as a pure metal. The moment of elation was short-lived, however. Almost simultaneously, a second telegram came through—informing her that Jeanne Langevin had released Marie's love letters to the press.

She abruptly left the conference and returned to France, where she faced notorious publicity. The press accused her of being a homewrecker, an immoral woman, and a Polish temptress. Anyone who tried to defend Marie—including Jean Perrin—toppled with her. At school, 14-year-old Irène got the news from a friend, who pointed to a headline about the affair in *L'Oeuvre* newspaper. After reading the story, she collapsed in tears. The ever-faithful Debierne picked Irène up and took her to the Borels, where Marie waited for her children. Noticing her mother's haggard state, Eve told Irène, "Mé (the name they called Marie) needs cuddling." Irène nestled in close to her beloved mother, and Marie, in a moment of rare affection, gently stroked Irène's hair.

Although some of her friends remained loyal, Paul Appell, like many others, turned his back on her. He even arranged for a group of professors at the Sorbonne to demand that she leave France. When Appell learned that his daughter Marguerite Borel had taken in Marie, he marched over to her house and told her that Marie must leave the country. Borel, who had never dared to argue with her father, firmly told him that if he drove Marie out

Marie Curie and Paul Langevin stand in front of a group of women in Paris around 1910, about the time the two began an intimate relationship. After Langevin's wife made Curie's love letters public, Curie was vilified in the press. Oddly enough, Langevin's behavior was never called into question.

of France, she would never speak to him again. Sensing she was serious, Appell gave in to his daughter's wishes and dropped his demand.

Borel pointed out what was oddly not obvious to the rest of society at the time. None of this would be happening if Marie were a man. No one had asked Langevin to leave the country. In fact, he was never even condemned for his actions. In those days, society looked the other way when men had affairs, but if a woman was caught doing the same, she was ruined. One daring journalist, Gustave Téry, did call Langevin "a boor and a coward." In anger, Langevin challenged him to a duel of pistols. Although illegal, duels were frequently fought. After a good show, Téry refused to fire his pistol, saying he did not want to kill one of France's greatest minds. Likewise, Langevin backed down.

Nevertheless, Jeanne Langevin's plan to destroy Marie could not have been more perfectly executed. The blow wrought irreversible damage, leaving behind a wounded and shattered Madame Curie. Shortly after the scandal broke, a member of the Nobel Committee sent Marie a letter, requesting that she not show up in Sweden to accept her prize. The reason he gave her, of course, was the published letters, and he added a stinging comment: "If the Academy had believed the letters . . . it would not, in all probability, have given you the Prize."[6] Undoubtedly, the harsh judgment needled Marie, and she boldly addressed the issue with a controversial response:

> You suggest to me . . . that the Academy of Stockholm, if it had been forewarned, would probably have decided not to give me the Prize, unless I could publicly explain the attacks of which I have been the object. . . . I must therefore act according to my convictions. . . . The action that you advise

would appear to be a grave error on my part. In fact the Prize has been awarded for discovery of Radium and Polonium. I believe that there is no connection between my scientific work and the facts of private life. . . . I cannot accept the idea in principle that the appreciation of the value of scientific work should be influenced by libel and slander concerning private life. I am convinced that this opinion is shared by many people.[7]

An outwardly proud and confident Marie Curie attended the Nobel ceremony, despite the warnings. Her sister Bronya and Irène accompanied her. King Gustaf awarded her the prize, and no one spoke a word about the affair. In her acceptance speech, Marie complimented other scientists who worked in the field of radioactivity but also firmly established her own credentials. Taking full credit for her accomplishments, she reminded those attending that the work of "isolating radium as a pure salt was undertaken by me alone."[8] Her speech rightfully put into place all male scientists who believed that any worthwhile work by a female scientist was done while working with a male colleague.

DID YOU KNOW?

Marie Curie was the first person to win or share two Nobel Prizes. She is one of only two people who have been awarded a Nobel Prize in two fields. The other laureate was Linus Pauling, who received prizes in chemistry and peace. Marie is the only person to have won the prize in two different *science* fields, and she is still the only woman to have won two Nobel Prizes.

Shortly after Marie returned to Paris, she was hospitalized with a kidney ailment. Some doctors thought the problem was caused by lesions pressing on her kidney. Still others diagnosed her with asymptomatic tuberculosis. No one mentioned, however, that she had experienced a total nervous breakdown and was slipping into the deepest, darkest depression of her life. Later, she confided in Eve that during this time she had wanted to kill herself. Undeniably, some of her letters indicate that she planned to commit suicide. She refused to eat, and her weight dropped from 123 pounds (56 kilograms) to a frail 103 pounds (47 kilograms). Eventually, the hospital sent her to the Sisters of the Family of Saint Marie, a facility that cared for patients who suffered from both medical and psychiatric problems. In February, she had a kidney operation. Convinced she was going to die, Marie gave explicit instructions to Debierne and Georges Gouy on how to dispose of her precious radium.

Marie gradually recovered. Meanwhile, Debierne tried to fill the gap at the Curie laboratory. He looked after Irène and Eve, writing Marie about every aspect of the children's lives. On Christmas in 1912, he told Marie that Eve was drastically sick. Marie made an amazing but temporary recovery so that she could travel to their new apartment on the Île St. Louis in Paris to be at her daughter's side. When Eve recovered, Marie left again. She remained too weak to resume her work on the radium standard, which had not yet been finished. Debierne forged on without her. Even from her sickbed, though, she was unwilling to hand the radium standard sample over to Rutherford. Finally, thanks to Debierne, she agreed to send the original if a duplicate sample could remain in the Curie laboratory. The original sample would then be moved to the Bureau of Weights and Standards in Sèvres. As promised, upon agreement of the compromise, the International Radium Standard Committee called the standard a "curie."

By July 1914, construction of the Curie laboratory, what would become the Radium Institute at the Pasteur Institute was almost complete. Marie was well enough to oversee the planting of trees and a rose garden between the two pavilions. It was more beautiful than she and Pierre could have ever imagined. Before the finishing touches could be made, though, there was yet another delay—World War I.

"Les Petites Curies"

On September 3, 1914, Marie Curie shuffled through the thick crowds at Paimpol Station in Paris, lugging a heavy suitcase. The German Army had invaded France and was advancing toward Paris. In her suitcase, Madame Curie carried France's national treasure—all the country's radium. Her mission was to transport the precious cargo to Bordeaux, where the French government had relocated.

After a 10-hour train trip, Marie arrived in Bordeaux, where a government official met her at the station. He drove her to a shabby little cottage, where she spent the night with her precious suitcase at the foot of the bed. The next morning, she was driven to the University of Bordeaux, and the radium was placed in a protective vault there. After the transfer, Marie was immediately taken back to the train station. She boarded a train full of soldiers who had been called to duty in Paris.

By the time Marie got back to Paris, the city was nearly deserted. Most people had fled to distant towns to escape the onslaught of the German Army. Marie detested war. As recorded in *Obsessive Genius*, she said, "Only through peaceful means can we achieve an ideal society. It is hard to think that after so many centuries of development, the human race still doesn't know how to resolve differences in any way except by violence."[1] Yet, she understood the real dangers of war and evacuated her daughters to l'Arcouëst with a governess. Almost 16, Irène watched over nine-year-old Eve. However, she did not enjoy her babysitting duties. Like her mother, Irène preferred to have her nose buried in a book, unbothered by mundane activities.

Scientists everywhere were experimenting with chemicals that might help their countries' militaries. They developed weapon uses for chlorine, mustard gas, and other deadly gases. One scientist invented a special fan that removed these poisonous gases from the trenches. Marie, too, wanted to help France, but not by any destructive means. Day after day, she watched maimed soldiers returning to Paris, limbs hacked off and lacerated by doctors digging around in the flesh to find bullets and shrapnel. On the battlefront, there were no technicians or X-ray equipment to treat the wounded properly. Marie sought to change this.

She devised an idea of a mobile X-ray unit that could be used in hospitals on the battlefront. To accomplish her ambition, she would need X-ray machines and cars. Within a few weeks, Marie had accumulated a stash of unused X-ray equipment from laboratories and clinics that had been shut down because of the war. The vehicle would have to be small enough to navigate narrow roads. A women's organization called the Union des Femmes de France

(Union of the Women of France) donated the first two cars. Each unit included a small generator that could be hooked up to the car battery when electricity was unavailable. Marie also installed an X-ray tube on a portable stand so the unit could be transported to the crucial area. Her ambulance was equipped with a folding examination table, photographic plates, heavy curtains to block out sunlight, and a screen. The first completed X-ray ambulance was officially named "Car E," but the units soon became known as "Les Petites Curies," or in English, "The Little Curies."

Marie made her first medical trip on November 1, 1914, taking Irène along as her assistant. Before long, Marie was needed in another area. Feeling that her daughter was capable of operating the equipment, Marie left 17-year-old Irène alone in charge of a field radiology facility in Hoogstade, Belgium. There, amid the thundering boom of cannon fire, Irène diligently aided wounded soldiers. Day after day, soldiers were carried in on stretchers, some dead, some without limbs, some with shattered bones, and some with skin cut to lace by shrapnel. The only trained technician, Irène X-rayed the wounded soldiers and then made a geometric calculation to pinpoint the exact location of the bullet or shrapnel. At first, the head surgeon stubbornly insisted on doing the X-rays himself, omitting Irène's crucial mathematical step. Too proud to consult a teenager, he blindly cut into the wounded soldiers. Unable to find the bullet and shrapnel, he randomly and mercilessly dug around the wound until he finally gave up and asked Irène for help.

On her eighteenth birthday, Irène wrote a letter to her mother, boasting that she had located four large shell fragments in a soldier's hand, which the surgeon then successfully removed. She spent that afternoon training nurses to take her place, because she was soon to be transferred to a new battlefield location. Irène's next station was at

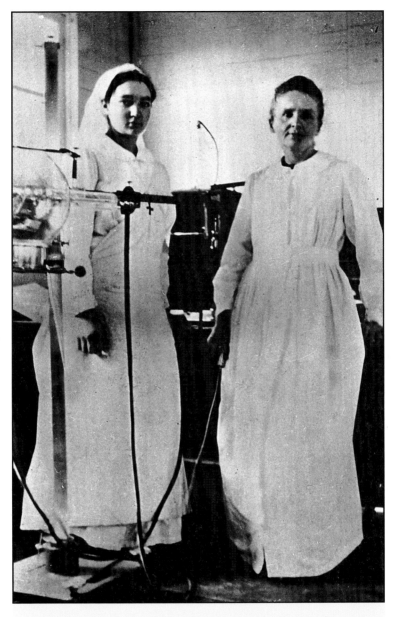

During World War I, Marie Curie developed a mobile X-ray unit so that X-rays of wounded soldiers could be taken on the battlefront. Her daughter Irène *(left)* learned how to work the equipment and then went on to train scores of X-ray technicians during the war.

Amiens. In Hoogstade, she had taught herself how to repair equipment, train nurses, and live like a soldier. In 1916, she returned to Paris to teach a training course for women X-ray technicians. By the end of the war, 150 technicians had been dispatched to various X-ray posts on the field. During this time, Irène attended the Sorbonne—just like her mother—and graduated with honors in mathematics, physics, and chemistry.

The Curie name was helping on other war fronts as well. At sea, the German submarines had proved lethal. By 1917, German subs had sunk 2,617 Allied ships. Paul Langevin, who had enlisted as an army sergeant, believed that he could use Pierre Curie's research in piezoelectricity to find a way to pick up sound waves beyond the range of the human ear. This type of technology would be useful in detecting undersea maneuvers. To help, Marie Curie loaned Langevin a piece of Pierre's piezoelectric quartz, which she had mounted on the wall of her office. Langevin recharged the quartz and used it to create a microphone that would capture ultrasonic vibrations like those that might be transmitted through seawater by submarines. By the middle of 1917, he had built a primitive apparatus that detected sounds with a wavelength as short as one ten-billionth of a millimeter. His device was the first sonar.

On November 11, 1918, Marie and Irène—Marie's new scientific partner—were working side by side in the laboratory of the recently completed Curie Institute. Suddenly, they heard the muffled sounds of cheering, music, and church bells coming from outside the laboratory windows. Throughout the streets of Paris, people were celebrating. After four bloody years, the Germans had been stopped and World War I was finally over. But for Marie, there would be more good news. During the Russian Revolution in 1917, Poland had briefly come under German control. With the defeat of the Germans, the war-ending Treaty of Versailles declared Poland an independent country. After 123 years of Russian rule, Poland was free. Surely Marie wished her father were still alive to share her excitement.

During the war, Marie had stayed true to her belief of using science to help people—not destroy them. Over the four-year period, more than a million X-ray procedures had been performed and thousands of lives were saved.

THAT MILLIONS SHALL NOT DIE

By the end of World War I, Marie's health had taken a serious decline. Poor eyesight left her nearly blind, and her anemia, caused by radiation, left her weak and listless. Still, she continued to work, with Irène as her faithful assistant. The French government offered her a small pension, which Marie accepted, but it did little to alleviate her money concerns. Other countries provided their scientists with much financial support, but not France. Marie desperately wanted to develop the reputation of her new institute and provide enough funds so that Irène could continue to work after she died.

In an incredible stroke of luck, Marie met her financial rescuer—Missy Meloney. Through her magazine *The Delineator*, Meloney went to work capturing the sympathies of Americans. In her articles, Meloney depicted Marie as utterly impoverished, so poor she could not afford the radium she needed to continue her valuable research for a cure for cancer. In truth, Marie lived quite comfortably in a spacious apartment on the Île St. Louis. She also was part owner of an apartment building and had bought vacation property in France. Because of Meloney's articles, few Americans understood that Marie actually needed more radium for research, not cancer treatments. Not to mention, in 1921, radium was used in cancer patients only as a last resort, primarily because it was so expensive. Radioactivity, Marie Curie's great discovery, was hard to explain and was

ATOMIC STRUCTURE

At the time the Curies discovered radioactivity, physicists believed that the atom was the ultimate, indivisible building block of matter. The discovery of radioactivity proved that atoms themselves must have structure and, therefore, were not the fundamental particles of nature. In 1911, Ernest Rutherford posited the existence of a nucleus within the atom by experiments in which alpha particles were scattered by thin metal foils. Since then, the nuclear hypothesis has grown into a refined and fully accepted theory of atomic structure. In this theory, the entire phenomenon of radioactivity can be explained.

Radioactivity refers to the particles that are emitted from nuclei as a result of nuclear instability. Many nuclear isotopes are unstable and emit some kind of radiation. The most common types of radiation are called alpha, beta, and gamma. The atom is believed to consist of a dense central nucleus surrounded by a cloud of electrons. The nucleus is made up of protons—equal to the number of electrons (in an electrically neutral atom) and neutrons. An alpha particle, which is a doubly charged helium ion, consists of two neutrons and two protons. Therefore, it can be emitted only from the nucleus of an atom. When a nucleus loses an alpha particle, a new nucleus is formed, lighter than the original by four mass units. For example, if an atom of uranium isotope with a mass of 238 emits an alpha particle, it becomes an atom of another element with a mass of 234. Because the charge on the uranium-238 nucleus decreases by two units, the atomic number is two less than the original, which is 92. The new atomic number is 90, an isotope of the element thorium.

By this method, Marie Curie was able to discover polonium and radium and place the new elements correctly on the atomic chart.

useless in gripping the emotions of Americans. Radium, however, was highly publicized, and diluted amounts of it were in all sorts of products, such as watch dials, beauty treatments, and hokey medicines. By the end of the articles, Meloney had all but promised a cure for cancer—found only through Marie and her radium.

Her first article was headlined "That Millions Shall Not Die." In the article, she pleaded with the American people to help Marie's cause. "The great Curie is getting older," she concluded, "and the world losing, God alone knows, what great secret. And millions are dying of cancer every year."[2] However exaggerated and fictionalized, Meloney's articles did the trick. One year later, Marie was aboard a boat for New York to pick up her $100,000 gift—a gram of radium.

Meloney had planned a rigorous schedule for the feeble Madame Curie, including 18 college lectures, the acceptance of seven honorary degrees, and a tour of Niagara Falls and the Grand Canyon. There were also countless dinners and lunches, as well as the final presentation—from the president himself on the steps of the White House. Marie was unable to keep up with the schedule. Too exhausted to travel, she stayed behind while her daughters toured the Grand Canyon. At last, she made it to the final dinner hosted by President Warren Harding followed by the symbolic presentation of the radium. In addition to the gram of radium, Marie received donated equipment from New York's Sloan Laboratory, $22,000 worth of mesothorium, $7,000 for giving lectures, an extra $52,000 that Meloney had raised, and another $50,000 from the Macmillian Company for publication rights to a biography of Pierre Curie, naturally to be written by Marie.

Despite the myth and melodrama, it seemed as though Marie's wish had come true. She now had the money to pass her legacy to Irène, certain no one could snatch her hard work away—especially her dear radium—after she

President Warren Harding spoke with Marie Curie during the 1921 ceremony in which a gift of one gram of radium was given to Curie. The American people raised money to purchase the radium after reading articles on Curie written by Missy Meloney, the editor of *The Delineator*.

was gone. Several years later, though, a handsome 25-year-old man would cause Marie to question the safety of her radium's future.

Passing the Torch

Since Pierre Curie's death, one thing in Marie's life seemed to give her happiness—her close working relationship with Irène. Ever since Irène was a little girl, Marie could see how much she was like her father. Perhaps working with Irène made Marie feel as though she was still close to Pierre. Realizing that her health was failing, Marie needed to pass the torch of her life's work to someone she could trust—she found this person in Irène. Naturally, Eve was somewhat jealous of Irène's relationship with Marie. For the most part, Eve and Irène were complete opposites. Quiet and cold, like her mother, Irène wore a plain white lab coat over her dark dress. She seemed so emotionless that people often referred to her as a "block of ice."[1] On the other hand, Eve, whom American papers hailed as "Eve of the radium eyes," dressed fashionably and wore eyeliner and bright red lipstick. Artistically gifted, Eve dreamed of being a concert pianist. When she practiced, Marie complained about the "noise."

In 1925, a nervous young man showed up at Marie's laboratory. His name was Frédéric Joliot. As a child, Frédéric had kept a photograph of the Curies taped on his bedroom wall. He had attended the School of Industrial Physics and Chemistry of the City of Paris (EPCI), where Pierre had once been a professor. Joliot studied under Paul Langevin, and it was Langevin who referred him to Marie. Under Langevin's recommendation, Marie hired the enthusiastic man to work at the institute. Unlike Irène and Marie, Frédéric was outgoing and energetic. At first, he felt isolated and alone in the silent, somber atmosphere of the laboratory. Gradually, though, he found himself becoming attracted to Irène. Throughout the year, they took long walks while they discussed work, much as Marie and Pierre had done.

One evening after being with Frédéric, Irène came home and announced, "Mé [mother], I'm engaged."[2] Marie was devastated by the news. She felt as though she was losing her loyal friend and partner and sole successor. She worried about the future of the Radium Institute. According to French law, husbands controlled their wives' property. If Irène married, she could lose control of the institute. Marie consulted a lawyer and made sure that Irène alone would inherit the institute's radium and other radioactive substances. On October 9, 1926, despite her mother's concerns, Irène and Frédéric were married. After a celebratory lunch, the newlyweds returned to the laboratory. In the beginning, Irène signed her papers "Irène Curie" and Frédéric signed his "F. Joliot." Soon, they both adjusted their last names to "Joliot-Curie." A year later, Irène gave birth to a daughter—Hélène.

In time, Marie warmed up to Frédéric, and she was pleased to see he was just as dedicated to radium research

Marie Curie enjoyed her close working relationship with her daughter Irène. Here, they are together in the lab in April 1927. Marie's other daughter, Eve, took care of Marie at the end of her life. After Marie's death, Eve wrote a popular biography of her mother.

as Irène was. In 1934, the couple discovered how to create artificial radioactivity, which one magazine called "one of the most important discoveries of the century."[3] In 1935, they received the Nobel Prize for their discovery. Irène Joliot-Curie became the second woman to receive a Nobel Prize in the sciences, after her mother. But Marie would not live to see it. As Irène and Frédéric showed Marie the results of their experiments, a look of great joy spread across her face. It was the last true moment of satisfaction in her life.

(continues on page 122)

CURIE'S DAUGHTERS

When delving into the life and work of Marie Curie, her daughter Irène takes the spotlight since she followed in her mother's footsteps with a love for science and radioactivity. In 1925, she received her doctorate of science, writing her thesis on the alpha rays of polonium—the element her mother discovered. Alone and in collaboration with her husband, Frédéric Joliot, she performed important work on natural and artificial radioactivity, transmutation of elements, and nuclear physics. In 1935, she shared the Nobel Prize in Chemistry with Frédéric for their discovery of artificial radioactivity.

Irène packed much work into her short 58-year life. In 1938, her research on the action of neutrons on the heavy elements became a crucial stepping stone to the discovery of uranium fission. She was a professor in the Faculty of Sciences at the Sorbonne in Paris until she took over as director of the Radium Institute in 1946. For six years, she was a Commissioner for Atomic Energy in France. She was appointed Undersecretary of the State for Scientific Research, was a member of several foreign academies and numerous scientific societies, held honorary doctorate degrees from several universities, and was an Officer of the Legion of Honour. In addition to her scientific work, she exercised a keen interest in the social and intellectual advancement of women and was a member of the World Peace Council.

Eve Curie also made amazing contributions to France and the world. At an early age, Eve became interested in music and the arts. For many years, she played piano. Like her sister, though, she also excelled in science. She graduated with honors with two bachelor degrees, one in science and one in philosophy, from

Sévigné College. Her dream of being a concert pianist came true in 1925, when she performed her first concert in Paris.

After her mother's death, Eve turned to writing. She decided to write a biography about Marie. In a tiny apartment in Auteuil, she shuffled through letters, papers, and other documents that belonged to her mother. During the fall of 1935, she journeyed to Poland, where she visited family and collected more information about Marie's childhood. In 1937, *Madame Curie* was published simultaneously around the world and quickly became a best seller in the United States.

In 1940, after the fall of France during World War II, she traveled to England and worked for the cause of Free France. Later, she became an officer of the women's division of the army and served in Europe with the Fighting French. She was appointed head of the feminine division of the Commissariat of Information. Articulate and eloquent, she served as the official spokesperson for the women of France during World War II.

In 1952, she was appointed Special Advisor to the Secretary General of NATO. On November 19, 1954, at age 49, she married Henry Richardson Labouisse, the U.S. ambassador to Greece. From 1962 to 1965, Eve served as the executive director of the United Nations Children's Fund for Greece. She and Labouisse also traveled to more than 100 of the developing nations under UNICEF relief.

On October 22, 2007, Eve died at her home in New York at the age of 102. According to her stepdaughter, Eve felt enormous guilt that, of the women in her family, she alone escaped a life of radiation and its consequences.

(continued from page 119)

MY CHILD

The ghastly realities of prolonged radiation exposure were not hidden secrets, even in the early years of discovery. The Curies took precautionary measures to protect their employees but did little to protect themselves. Pierre and Marie even kept a vial of radium salts at their bedside so they could fall asleep beneath its dazzling glow. Over the years, recurrent radium burns caused the skin on Marie's fingers to become stiff, split, and calloused, like deep cracks in dry red clay. Her fingertips had gone numb, and she habitually rubbed them together trying to awaken them. Years of radiation had seeped into Marie's bones, damaging the marrow and causing her to become ill.

In May 1934, Marie visited her laboratory for the last time. She left around 3:30 in the afternoon, complaining of a headache, fever, and chills. Eve, the child she had shut out, became her nurse and devoted companion. Marie was admitted to the Sancellemoz, a hospital in Haute-Savoie Mont-Blanc in the French Alps. In the last months of her life, Marie suffered terribly. At times, Eve had to leave the room, because she could not bear to see her mother in such agony. On July 2, Irène and Frédéric arrived to visit Marie. The next morning, Marie's temperature dropped. Looking out the open window, sunlight sparkling on the snowy mountaintops, Marie said, "It wasn't the medicine that made me better. It was the pure air, the altitude."[4] Any hopes for a miraculous recovery, however, were abruptly dashed. Later that day, she fell into a deep coma. At dawn, on July 4, 1934, as the sun rose in a flawless sky, Marie took her final breath. In Marie's final moments, Eve was the only daughter at her bedside. Irène was too distraught to stay in the room.

The death of 66-year-old Madame Curie made front-page news around the world. Her doctor ruled her death a form of anemia, caused from years of radiation that affected

In 1995, the coffins containing the ashes of Marie and Pierre Curie were transferred for entombment at the Panthéon in Paris. The Panthéon holds the remains of great Frenchmen like Voltaire, Jean-Jacques Rousseau, and Victor Hugo. Marie Curie was the first woman to be enshrined at the Panthéon.

her bones and prevented her from reacting normally to the disease. She was buried next to her beloved Pierre in Sceaux, and her body rested there for 61 years until their ashes were transferred to the Panthéon in Paris.

Irène followed in her mother's footsteps right until the end. She died in 1956 at age 58 of leukemia contracted by exposure to radioactive materials. Frédéric died two years later. In morbid humor, he called their illness an "occupational disease."[5]

Many people wonder how Marie Curie could have exposed herself and her precious daughter to the devastating effects of radiation. They used their naked hands to perform experiments and shockingly transferred radium and polonium from one container to another by sucking up the substances with a pipette. As strange as it may sound, Marie probably did so out of love—love for science, love for discovery, and love for the world by trying to make it a better place. Marie called radium "my child." In fact, it was. Her work gave birth to a whole new field of scientific study. Although logical and meticulous, she viewed her research as a delicate rose—a thing of brilliance. "I am among those who think that science has great beauty," she once said. "A scientist in his laboratory is not only a technician, he is also a child placed before natural phenomena which impress him like a fairy tale."[6]

CHRONOLOGY

1867   Marya Sklodowska is born on November 7 in Warsaw, Poland.

1874   Oldest sister, Zosia, dies of typhus.

1878   Marie's mother, Bronislava, dies of tuberculosis on May 9.

1883   Graduates from high school and receives a gold medal for her outstanding academic success.

1885–1889   Works as a governess.

1891   Enrolls as a student at the Sorbonne in Paris, France.

1893   Earns her master's degree in physics, becoming the first woman to graduate at the top of the class.

1894   Meets Pierre Curie; earns her master's degree in mathematics, scoring second-highest in the class.

1895   Marries Pierre Curie on July 26.

1897   First daughter, Irène, is born on September 12.

1898   Focuses her research on the study of Becquerel rays, a newly developed process; as a result, the Curies discover radioactivity, radium, and polonium.

1903   The Curies are awarded the Nobel Prize in Physics for discovering radioactivity and the Davy Medal of the Royal Society; Marie becomes head of the physics lab at the Sorbonne and earns her Doctor of Science degree.

1904   Second daughter, Eve, is born on December 6.

1906   Pierre is killed after being hit by a horse-drawn wagon on April 19.

1910   Marie publishes her two-volume *Treatise on Radioactivity*.

1911   Receives her second Nobel Prize, this time in chemistry, for her discovery of radium and polonium.

1914   Invents a mobile X-ray unit to help wounded soldiers on the front during World War I; appointed director of the Curie laboratory in the Radium Institute.

1921   Travels to the United States, where President Warren Harding presents her with a gram of radium.

1934   Dies on July 4 from complications due to overexposure to radiation throughout her scientific career.

NOTES

CHAPTER 1: "CURIE CURES CANCER!"

1. Denis Brian, *The Curies: A Biography of the Most Controversial Family in Science*. Hoboken, N.J.: John Wiley & Sons, 2005, p. 180
2. Ann Lewicki, MD, MPH, "Marie Sklodowska Curie in America, 1921." Department of Radiology, Georgetown University School of Medicine, Washington, D.C., August 2, 2001. Available online at http://radiology.rsnajnls.org/cgi/content/full/223/2/299.

CHAPTER 2: MANYA: A BRILLIANT CHILD

1. Barbara Goldsmith, *Obsessive Genius: The Inner World of Marie Curie*. New York: Atlas Books, W.W. Norton & Company, 2005, p. 25.
2. Ibid., p. 27.
3. Ibid., p. 27.

CHAPTER 3: GOVERNESS

1. Brian, *The Curies*, p. 25.
2. Ibid., p. 26.
3. Ibid., p. 28.
4. Susan Quinn, *Marie Curie: A Life*. New York: Simon & Schuster, 1995, p. 75.
5. Brian, *The Curies*, p. 30.
6. Goldsmith, *Obsessive Genius*, p. 49.
7. Brian, *The Curies*, p. 38.

CHAPTER 4: SETTING THE STAGE

1. Goldsmith, *Obsessive Genius*, p. 54.
2. Brian, *The Curies*, p. 40.
3. Ibid., p. 42.
4. Ibid., p. 43.
5. Goldsmith, *Obsessive Genius*, p. 65.

CHAPTER 5: A YEAR OF GREAT DISCOVERIES

1. Ibid., p. 77.
2. Brian, *The Curies*, p. 58.
3. Goldsmith, *Obsessive Genius*, p. 88.

CHAPTER 6: OBSESSED WITH RADIUM

1. Ibid., p. 96.
2. Ibid., p. 100.
3. Ibid., p. 94.
4. Ibid., p. 96.
5. Ibid., p. 97.
6. Brian, *The Curies*, p. 70.

CHAPTER 7: LONELY SCIENTIST

1. Goldsmith, *Obsessive Genius*, p. 115.
2. Marie Curie, *Pierre Curie*. New York: Macmillan Co., 1923, pp. 127–128.
3. Quinn, *Marie Curie*, pp. 219–220.
4. Goldsmith, *Obsessive Genius*, p. 128
5. Ibid., p. 133.
6. Brian, *The Curies*, p. 100.
7. Eve Curie, *Madame Curie*. New York: Doubleday, Doran & Company, Inc., 1937, p. 247.
8. Brian, *The Curies*, p. 103.
9. Goldsmith, *Obsessive Genius*, p. 140.
10. Ibid.
11. Brian, *The Curies*, p. 108.
12. Goldsmith, *Obsessive Genius*, p. 150.

CHAPTER 8: A BETTER WORLD

1. Ibid., p. 154.
2. Ibid., p. 155
3. Ibid., p. 166.
4. Ibid., p. 167.
5. Ibid., pp. 169–170.

6. Ibid., p. 177.
7. Ibid., pp. 177–178.
8. Ibid., p. 178.

CHAPTER 9: "LES PETITES CURIES"

1. Ibid., pp. 185–186.
2. Ibid., p. 193.

CHAPTER 10: PASSING THE TORCH

1. Brian, *The Curies*, p. 200.
2. Goldsmith, *Obsessive Genius*, p. 206.
3. Ibid., p. 213.
4. Brian, *The Curies*, p. 250.
5. Goldsmith, *Obsessive Genius*, p. 219.
6. Ibid., p. 233.

BIBLIOGRAPHY

Brian, Denis. *The Curies: A Biography of the Most Controversial Family in Science*. Hoboken, N.J.: John Wiley & Sons, 2005.

Curie, Eve. *Madame Curie*. New York: Doubleday, Doran & Company, Inc., 1937.

Curie, Marie. *Pierre Curie*. New York: Macmillan Co., 1923.

Curie, Marie. *Radioactive Substances*. New York: Philosophical Library, 1961.

Fox, Margalit. "Eve Curie Labouisse, Mother's Biographer, Dies at 102." *New York Times*, October 25, 2007. Available online at http://www.nytimes.com/2007/10/25/arts/25labouisse.html.

Goldsmith, Barbara. *Obsessive Genius: The Inner World of Marie Curie*. New York: Atlas Books, W.W. Norton & Company, 2005.

Lewicki, Ann, MD, MPH. "Marie Sklodowska Curie in America, 1921." Department of Radiology, Georgetown University School of Medicine, Washington, D.C., August 2, 2001. Available online at http://radiology.rsnajnls.org/cgi/content/full/223/2/299.

Marie Curie and the Science of Radioactivity Web site. Available online at http://www.aip.org/history/curie/contents.htm.

Nobel Prize Web site. Available online at http://nobelprize.org.

Pflaum, Rosalynd. *Grand Obsession: Madame Curie and Her World*. New York: Doubleday, 1989.

Preston, Diana. *Before the Fallout: From Marie Curie to Hiroshima*. New York: Walker, 2005.

Quinn, Susan. *Marie Curie: A Life*. New York: Simon & Schuster, 1995.

FURTHER RESOURCES

BOOKS

Hall, Linley Erin. *Who's Afraid of Marie Curie? The Challenges Facing Women in Science and Technology*. Berkeley, Calif.: Seal Press, 2007.

McClafferty, Carla Killough. *Something Out of Nothing: Marie Curie and Radium*. New York: Farrar, Straus & Giroux, 2006.

McGrayne, Sharon Bertsch. *Nobel Prize Women in Science: Their Lives, Struggles, and Momentous Discoveries*. Washington, D.C.; Joseph Henry Press, 2001.

Ogilvie, Marilyn Bailey. *Marie Curie: A Biography*. Westport, Conn.: Greenwood Press, 2004.

Pasachoff, Naomi. *Marie Curie and the Science of Radioactivity*. New York: Oxford University Press, 1997.

WEB SITES

Institut Curie
  http://www.curie.fr/fondation/index.cfm/lang/_gb.htm

Marie Curie and the Science of Radioactivity
  http://www.aip.org/history/curie/contents.htm

Nobel Prize
  http://nobelprize.org

INDEX

ABOUT THE AUTHOR

RACHEL A. KOESTLER-GRACK has worked with nonfiction books as an editor and writer since 1999. During her career, she has worked extensively with historical topics, ranging from the Middle Ages to the colonial era to the civil rights movement. In addition, she has written numerous biographies on a variety of historical and contemporary figures. Rachel lives with her husband and daughter in the German community of New Ulm, Minnesota.

PICTURE CREDITS